THE BOOK OF
SWEETS

THE BOOK OF SWEETS

MARINA SCHINZ

Harry N. Abrams, Inc., Publishers

For Cady and Tom

My Mother, Smoking a Candy Cigar; Naples, 1916
Box of Chocolate Cigars; 4″ long. Milan

Page 1: Gingerbread Hearts and Children; Boy and girl: 6½″ high. Patty Paige, New York

Page 2: Lovers, Anise Cookie; 5½ x 2¾″. Switzerland.
Sugar Confections; Includes gingerbread, chocolate, marzipan, sugar paste. Size range: ½–5½″

Contents

Introduction

SUGAR is a thrilling substance. Its consumption produces a delectable sensation and its physiological satisfaction is instant and addictive—the very opposite of an acquired taste. The pursuit of this intense pleasure is usually an infant's first passion, a love which often strikes with a force to last a lifetime and which is responsible for our earliest "soft spot," the sweet tooth. Everybody is familiar with the seductive power of a piece of candy persuasively offered up as a reward or a bribe long before other value systems have been introduced into a child's life. Language reflects this connection as well: the Indo-European root *swad* is in fact the origin of both the words *sweet* and *persuade*.

Not only are children partial to a sweet taste; animals love it too. Bears hunt for it, horses relish it, some exotic birds devour it, bees treasure it. And where humans—often adult males—profess that they do not care for the stuff, they nevertheless call their girlfriends "sugar" and their spouses "honey" and generally feel that love is sweet. On every level sweetness is the expression of all that is delicious and exquisite in life.

Sugar, or sucrose, an organic chemical of the carbohydrate family, is an integral part of all green plants. The crystalline substance extracted from sugar cane (*Saccharaum officinarum L.*), once extremely rare, was originally imported to Europe from the Middle East as a spice. For many centuries it was administered as medicine; sometimes it still

is. Like salt, sugar keeps indefinitely. In high enough concentration it kills bacteria and its preservative properties are phenomenal, extending the life span of fruit and other perishable foods by months or years, enhancing their flavor without risk to our health.

It seems noteworthy that we cannot harm ourselves with sugar as we can with salt. Apparently, an old Chinese form of suicide consisted of ingesting two pounds of the latter, which resulted in an agonizing death by dehydration. With sugar we can happily indulge ourselves without fatal results—not that doctors or dentists would recommend doing so. Nevertheless sugar is the only chemical substance that we can eat by the spoonful in practically pure form.

Nor is this the extent of sugar's virtues. For not only is its taste sheer bliss, it is also the most versatile ingredient in our pantry, whose physical transformations border on magic. With a little moisture sugar can be pressed into rough lumps, smooth tablets, geometric cubes, or cone-shaped loaves, each hard as rock, whereas with the addition of heat it can be spun into gossamer threads, or poured to resemble the consistency of glass. It is thus a decorative material with broad applications. When mixed with other ingredients such as dough, nuts, egg white, chocolate, or plant gums, the result is an even greater multitude of artistic medias, which in turn can be sculpted, modeled, chiseled, cast, assembled, or "glued." Once fashioned into the desired shape, the sweet confection can be glazed, painted, airbrushed, or stenciled. The wide variety of techniques supplies confectioners with unlimited creative possibilities.

Not surprising, therefore, is the diverse iconography of the sweetmaker's art, which ranges from the bizarre or humorous to the religious, and from the erotic to the patriotic. As we see the procession of seasonal sweets that pass through candy kitchens and fill shop windows, we realize there is hardly an animal or manmade item that has not been cast in dough, marzipan, or chocolate. These edible objects, rich in flavor, calories, and folklore, are characterized by a strong element of fantasy, giving rise to the speculation that their enigmatic charm may go beyond the merely decorative. Such sweets are generally affixed to a particular season or a specific date. Carnival and Easter, All Saints and All Souls Day, Christmas and the Epiphany are all festivities rooted in the cycles of agriculture and nature, and have long stimulated the production of foods with symbolic meaning. Likewise the milestones of human life—birth, the coming of age, marriage, and death—are rich occasions for bakers and confectioners, who celebrate these highlights of the social calendar with cakes and cookies, chocolates and ice cream, sweetmeats and candies, usually adorned with or disguised as emblems of fecundity.

It is this particular facet of the confectioner's art that this book hopes to explore by showing the most accomplished or amusing sweets, whose craftsmanship is particularly touching, considering it is rendered in ephemeral merchandise meant for consumption within hours or days of its completion. Short of eating these attractive and sometimes strange objects, photography seems the most appropriate way to do them justice. The confections reproduced here were gathered quite casually over a period of about fifteen years. Their representation has not been based on any sort of systematic search, but reveals a personal choice whose selection process is best compared to grazing.

Some people have expressed surprise that a photographer of gardens should fall on such an esoteric and seemingly far-out subject, one which they presume to be totally unrelated to my main activities. One friend in particular is convinced that I chose this turf largely to immerse myself in sugar, but if that were the case I would have tackled a comprehensive encyclopedia of desserts, photographing and tasting myriads of pastries and puddings in abstract shapes, often with such amusing names as *Malakoff, syllabubs,* and *nun's poops.* As it is, I opted for a much narrower sector of sweets, namely that of representational objects. For these intriguing artifacts spoke to me, and did so in a language of their own: much like hieroglyphs they imply meaning, but more often than not I have enjoyed them for their sheer appearance. A closer study of sweets reveals that the confections produced today are only a fraction of the goods produced in the past. As it turns out, our sweets have a firm cultural heritage and constitute a delightful aspect of popular culture and art history—whimsical and frivolous though it may be, but history nonetheless.

As for a link to the world of horticulture, which is my main passion, it exists, if even loosely. Many of the sweets portrayed are strictly seasonal and often come in the shape of fruit and flowers, which are the confectioner's most popular motifs: Flora and Demeter decidedly assisted as the godmothers to this decorative craft. What is a less obvious but equally valid tie to the world of gardens and agriculture is that nearly all the substances used in the creation of crafted sweets are derived from plants, some of them quite unusual. And finally, there is the intrinsic perishability of gardens and most confections, both of which seem worth preserving, not only to document the past but above all to provide inspiration for the future. Creative efforts put into such fleeting moments of perfection have always touched and delighted me, and seem worth preserving.

Gingerbread

HONEY cakes and gingerbreads make their appearance when the sun is low and the day are short and glum. As the winter solstice draws closer we seek to lift our spirits with comfort and joy and we crave the carbohydrates which keep our bodies warm. Many baked goods have sprung up over the ages in answer to these needs and are typical for this time of the year which Christianity has appropriated as its own. The six weeks nestled around Christmas abound with sweets and delicacies often lavishly decorated with sunbursts, sheaves of wheat, clusters of fruits and flowers, in short, not with religious motifs but with symbols of regeneration, rebirth, and fertility. Although the world of sweets is a rich repository of recipes that have been perpetuated by tradition, often consumers (and sometimes creators) have been unaware of their origin or meaning. For while we sink our teeth into a sweet warm bun or nibble on a fragrant cinnamon star, anthropology is not what we have foremost on our mind.

The season to be jolly was instated long before the church decreed in 356 A.D. that Christ was born on December 25. Many of our feasts are the successors of pagan celebrations, rites of spring, and harvest festivals, and much of the imagery connected with our church holidays has ancient roots. The druidical Teutons, to quote just one example, were sun worshippers; as a forest people they were also given to the veneration of trees. Their Yule was a twelve-day celebration in the dead of winter, and it is to them that we owe not only the Christmas tree but the word jolly (from Yule) as well.

HONEY CAKES
Car: 9 x 15 x 1"; cat: 11 x 6 x 1"; carriage: 9 x 15 x 1".
Belgium

This assortment of large honey cakes, manufactured by a firm with an extensive collection of wooden molds, is made from flour and honey. Like hardtack, these cakes have to be broken and dunked in tea or coffee before they become edible.

The humble little gingerbread man has an equally inspired provenance, for just as the suggestive aroma of this droll cookie is apt to conjure up long-forgotten childhood memories, his simple shape and seasonal appearance point in the direction of a more primitive past. While his precise origin is lost to us now, his roots may be traced back to the dawn of our culture when the burying of the old year was usually celebrated with fire and dance rituals, with orgiastic activities, and with pleas to heathen gods—and especially goddesses—for fertile crops and stables during the upcoming year. Although perhaps apocryphal, it has been suggested that our pagan foremothers made decidedly male shapes out of dough, which they would throw into bonfires as part of their ritualistic dances.

To fully comprehend the meaning and impact of figuratively shaped food we gain further insight by looking back to the time when our prehistoric ancestors moved from a nomadic existence as hunters and gatherers and became settlers, intent on shepherding and farming. In those Neolithic days (3000–1800 B.C.), people labored very hard to make the grains they harvested edible and digestible. Barley, millet, and in the north oats and rye, were toasted and ground to a coarse flour, which then had to be moistened with some liquid before it could be eaten. For a considerable period of time, such grain foods were civilization's main staples. It was the heating or baking of this cereal (however accidental) that resulted in a kind of unleavened bread. Leavened bread, also undoubtedly was a chance discovery, and was probably made by the Egyptians, successful brewers who had started to cultivate wheat and are credited with having invented the oven. Although the first written document on wheat in Egypt dates from 2650 B.C., its actual cultivation may be several thousand years earlier. This new cereal yielded a much finer flour than other grains, and on account of its gluten content was eminently suitable for making bread. The malleability of this elastic dough must have been irresistible to our playful and ingenious ancestors. And since heat for baking, which we naively take for granted today, was not all that easy to come by, baked goods were a luxury. Indeed, from its inception bread had status and was more desirable than the polentas and porridges, gruels and pulses that were the daily fare of the general population.

Throughout history, bread has had great symbolic importance for agrarian cultures and was often thought to endow certain mystical powers. These powers were sometimes enhanced by mixing dough with unusual ingredients or by giving it a specific shape. The latent magic strength of such food would presumably extend itself to the person who ate it or employed it for some sacrificial use. Animal shapes were particularly important because they could be substituted for living creatures in sacrifices to the gods whose favors were sought or whose anger had to be appeased. One theory holds that bread baked in the form of a braid may have been a substitute for human hair, which in turn was assumed to be a replacement for a human head. Many of the woven, braided, plaited, and twisted bread forms had the power to summon good fortune; moreover, some were even powerful enough to ban evil altogether. In medieval Germany, pentagrams were carved into the threshold of houses to keep the devil away. Maybe the pretzel had a similar task.

The history of actual images used by bakers and confectioners goes back quite far and is sustained by archaeological finds, such as the molds used to shape dough or seals to make imprints with. The oldest of these were found in the Indus valley and are believed to represent the sun. The royal residence of Mari in Mesopotamia (1800 B.C.) had a tiled bakery containing about fifty molds elaborately decorated with animal scenes and geometric ornaments. Ancient Egyptian baked goods came in many forms, including stars, flowers, lions, calves, oxen, fish, and even a hippopotamus. By

OFFLETE
8″ diameter, ¹⁄₁₆″ thick. Zurich

TIRGGEL
3½ x 5″, 2½ x 2″. Zurich

These Offlete (i.e., waffles) and Tirggel are
not only the thinnest but also the oldest
extant sweets that bear images. Both were
originally Christmas or winter confections.
While the crisp, paper-thin Offlete is
fragile, the Tirggel is a durable, hard, flour-
and-honey cookie.

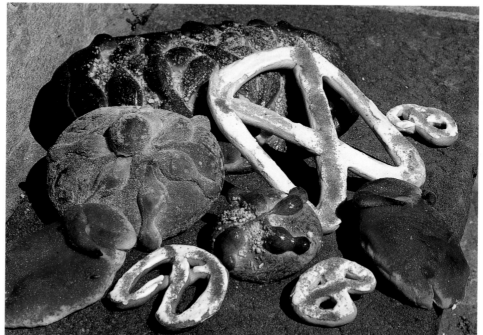

MEXICAN BREADS
(PAN DE LOS MUERTES)
Largest loaf: 10 x 16 x 5″;
smallest pretzel: 3½ x 3½″

Sweet breads, made for Mexico's Day of
the Dead (Dia de los Muerte) are decorated with designs inspired by the human
skeleton, one of the country's favorite motifs. Interesting is the introduction of the
color red, one of the most powerful symbols, standing for blood or, in this context,
for the blazing fires of hell.

Wir sind zwei Narren
unter einem Hut.
Der Dritte uns
beschauen tut.

Ich gehe in der Welt herum
und mache alte Weib', jung.

Der Klaus bringt
Kindern, artig u.
feineinen Christ-
-baum hinein.

Ihr Jungfern greifet hurtig an
die Teige kriegt keinen Mann
es mag doch spitter nicht geraun
die Teigen müssen fostik blaun

TIRGGEL
5 x 3½". Zurich

TIRGGEL
5 x 3½". Zurich

The repertory of gingerbread images grew steadily over the centuries. The depiction of the human figure, such as this courtly musician carrying a harp, made from a 19th-century mold, was a favorite subject of the lebkuchen trade. Queen Elizabeth I, who apparently loved sweets and suffered from bad teeth, had her courtiers portrayed in gingerbread.

This cookie made from a turn-of-the-century mold depicts the marital woes of an angry housewife retrieving her husband from the tavern with what appears to be a rolling pin. The caption, translated as "How Babs gets her husband out of the pub," may refer to the fact that the word Tirggel was slang for drunkenness.

(OPPOSITE) FOUR TIRGGEL
5 x 3½". Zurich

All these cookies were made from 19th-century wooden molds. Captions, riddles, proverbs, or moral instruction were quite common on this type of honey cookie, as well as on waffles. UPPER LEFT: A magician in whimsical garb, advertising his ability to rejuvenate old women. UPPER RIGHT: Two fools in Commedia del'Arte costumes. LOWER LEFT: An antique Saint Nicholas or "man-in-the-woods" dressed in furry clothes, carrying a Christmas tree for good children. LOWER RIGHT: Spinsters picking husbands from a "bridegroom tree."

500 B.C., the ancient Greeks were proficient bakers: they had the first commercial bakeries (which also employed women), and produced many different types of bread. Jerusalem at about the same time had a bread factory and a bakers' guild, while Rome boasted a special market for sweets, the *forum cupedinis,* supplied by *dulciarii* and *pistores candidarii.* Pliny the Elder, the invaluable source for the details of cultural life, reports that good children were rewarded with honey cakes representing one of the gods of Olympus. The molds surviving from 200 A.D. depict images of games, chariot races, theatrical scenes, and wild animals.

To be a baker was already a much esteemed profession in Roman times and we must assume that this was the case throughout the early Middle Ages, although the hiatus on culinary and other information between antiquity and 1200 A.D. shrouds most aspects of daily life in darkness. Bread was still reserved for the wealthy even after the enlightened monarch Charlemagne decided that every district had to have its own baker. Apparently this did not diminish the status of the baker, considering the fact that the *Sachsenspiegel,* a German law code, stipulated four hundred years later that the reparation to be paid for murdering a baker was three times as high as that for an ordinary citizen.

As bread became more widely available its symbolic value was extended to honey cakes and gingerbreads, which were made of dough variously enriched with honey, nuts, and spices. The church played a vital role in the creation and distribution of these gingerbreads. Monasteries were havens of peacetime activities where the tasks of good husbandry were attended to. Horticulture went hand in hand with early pharmacology and especially beekeeping, which had the dual purpose of providing candlewax for the church and honey, which for all practical purposes was the sweetener until about 1700 A.D., sugar being extremely scarce and astronomically priced. Monastery kitchens were often the workshops for new creations, where honey was put to good use by monks and nuns as medicine, mead, and in honey cakes. The ecclesiastical records and documents which keep us informed about the goings-on of those early days often contained reports by local prelates lamenting the heathen conditions they encountered. In particular, they denounced and condemned baked goods in the shape of pagan idols and those of witches and so-called scurrilous representations. Where the church could not erase certain deep-rooted customs, it usurped and adapted them. Thus, at the Pope's suggestion, church holidays were made to coincide with popular feasts. On these special days markets were set up in the neighborhood of heathen places of worship where monks sold off their merchandise, such as saints, molded in gingerbread, beautifully decorated and magnificently gilded.

It is interesting to look at this cunning move in the light of modern advertising. Christianity competed in a direct way with other religions, trying to outdo its competitors just as a modern company would. In an effort to lure followers of other religions into its own camp it countered its enemy's imagery by introducing its own signs and symbols. "We try harder" would have been a very appropriate slogan for the church in the sixth century. Indeed, in more recent centuries

HONEY CAKE
Lady: 26 x 10 x 1½"; dog: 9 x 15 x 1". Belgium

This oversized cookie, in the shape of an 18th-century lady and romantically inscribed as Le Matin de la Vie, *is very different from the typical burlesque characters in Flemish gingerbread tradition.*

V.COLLARD
DINANT

LE MATIN DE LA VIE.

TERRA-COTTA MOLD WITH SPRINGERLE COOKIE
4½ x 2″. Southern Germany

*Fired clay molds flourished from 1600–1800; this one, producing a baroque gentleman im-
printed on an anise cookie, dates from the late 18th century. Surprisingly, some of the older
terra-cotta molds have survived their wooden counterparts, which have a tendency to rot.*

(OPPOSITE) LARGE ANISE COOKIE
6″ diameter, ¾″ thick. Zurich

*The mold for this cookie, depicting the wheat harvest, was carved for the bakers' guild in
Zurich during the second half of the 17th century. The cookies or small cakes made from it
were given away by guild members as New Year's gifts or consumed at christenings, weddings,
and funerals.*

GINGERBREAD HORSE
11 x 14 x ¼". United States

This gingerbread horse with simple icing was made after a Russian lebkuchen design from Arkhangelesk, a town on the White Sea. In the gingerbread department it is one of many examples of images traveling far from home.

BERNER BÄR
Bear; 5 x 8 x ¾". Switzerland

A hazelnut-based honey cake features Bern's heraldic animal. Formerly only produced at Christmas time, it has now become a year-round confection because of its attraction to tourists.

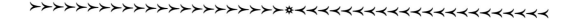

sweets became a welcome vehicle for what today is known as advertising and public relations.

Thanks to the church's entrepreneurial instincts circa 600–700 A.D., gingerbread has been a standard fairground treat. In medieval England, gingerbread was made to look like fashionable leather armor, with gilded cloves for nails and box leaves forming a fleur de lys design, further evoking the merriment of country fairs with their jousting tournaments and dancing bears, where these confections were sold. Eventually these heraldic patterns were replaced by frilly sugar icing and later still by paper stickers. "To take the gilt off the gingerbread" is an expression still used in England when referring to something that has been stripped of its most attractive feature.

With the progression of the Middle Ages the production of gingerbread became an independent profession. The *Lebzelters,* or gingerbread makers as they were called in German-speaking countries, were also candle makers, often using the molds they carved for wax as well as for sweets, steadily increasing their store of biblical, mythological, and profane images. The fact that gingerbread is made from a slab of dough which takes an imprint well adds an extra dimension to its basic attraction. Although gingerbread shapes can be made freehand or with the aid of a stencil, gingerbread's historical value lies in its ability to render the images carved in wood or modeled in ceramic molds. It is only thanks to the existence of a large number of old molds that we have a precise idea of what the gingerbreads of the past looked like.

Basically, gingerbread making was a Northern and cold-weather craft. Carving lebkuchen molds became a flourishing folk art from 1600 on, as judged from the many museum pieces found throughout Northern, Central, and Eastern Europe. Hungary in particular had masterful carvers and stands out with an extraordinary collection of wooden molds worthy of the historians' attention for their craftsmanship, rich imagery, and documentation of bygone days. The tastiest lebkuchen often came from crossroads of the spice trade or regions particularly rich in honey, such as Nuremberg, which was called "the bee garden of Europe."

A counterpart to the gingerbread type cookies which also required molds were the somewhat fragile and ephemeral waffles, wafers, *gaufres,* and *oblaten* or *offleten.* These sweets pertained to carnival, as can be seen, for example, in Pieter Brueghel's painting *The Battle Between Carnival and Lent.* Waffles are made by pouring a rich egg batter onto a piping hot hinged double iron with long handles, which has first been brushed with butter. After Shrove Tuesday—the day many deep-fried sweets were enjoyed for one last binge before Lent—waffles were replaced by water pretzels. These waffle irons, which flourished between 1600–1800, are the most exquisite and ornate of all tools; as such, they were often part of the dowry of wealthy young ladies. Their rich iconography and superb engraving technique, comparable to the goldsmith's art, is so remarkable that one cannot help but think that the waffle itself must have been an incidental byproduct of the tool that had been designed for the purpose. Apart from biblical scenes, they depicted family crests, vignettes of daily life, and peasant idylls, often with captions and verses.

In Zurich in the 1950s, there was still a genuine waferer called the *Hüppen Deppeler,* who had taken over this honorable trade from his father and had practiced his craft in a small, dark workshop in the old part of town. He made nothing else but *Offleten* and *Hüppen,* using the traditional irons belonging to old local families. With his death in the 1960s a time-honored specialized craft and an entire era came to an end.

Gingerbread stands for a variety of flattish cakes or cookies in fanciful shapes. Initially they were made with a mixture of flour, honey, and some spice. Gradually this basic recipe was enriched by the addition of butter, an occasional egg, candied fruit, and sugar. The distinctive taste of these

BUDDHA
10 x 7 x 1½". New York

FISH
7 x 10 x 1½". Chinatown, New York

This hard almond cake, produced in New York's Chinatown from a Chinese wooden mold, is the Buddha of Double Happiness. Character-ized by the heart-shaped red stamps, it is made for weddings. The necklace the Buddha wears is supposedly fashioned from the seeds of the tree of life, promising happiness, prosperity, and longevity.

As a symbol, the fish is one of the most universal. In China it stands for abundance of every kind, including wealth and honor. The red plum blossom stamp means luck.

(OPPOSITE) BREAD MASK
14 x 11 x 3". Basel, Switzerland

A bread mask of sweet yeast dough represents the Lällekeenig, one of the emblems and landmarks of the city of Basel. Masks are important objects in Swiss mountain cultures, acting as shields to ward off evil.

PLAYING CARDS
United States and Switzerland

GOLD AND SILVER CHOCOLATE COINS
United States and Switzerland

Christmas elicits colorful and toylike confections, such as these playing cards in lebkuchen with marzipan faces from Switzerland, and butter cookies from New York decorated with edible decals. The Swiss banknote is a chocolate painting on a filled wafer biscuit. The gold bars and coins in foil wrappers are links to the legend of Saint Nicholas, who dropped off bags of gold at the house of three poor maidens, thus providing them with a dowry that saved them from a life of prostitution.

baked goods is largely determined by the spices that go into them. Europe's appetite for exotic ingredients was uncontrollable once the Crusaders had shown the way and conspicuous consumption became rampant. Thus festive cooking and baking among the wealthy was synonymous with wanton use of the spice box. Cinnamon, cardamom, nutmeg, mace, coriander, ginger, and pepper allowed for different combinations, some of which were reflected in their names, such as the French *pain d'epices* and the German *Pfefferkuchen*. Every self-respecting town and every housewife had a special recipe. The Anglo-Saxon countries created their own brand by replacing the honey with molasses or treacle and gave ginger permanent center stage. Unlike other cookies, gingerbread and lebkuchen do not taste their best when they come straight out of the oven, but improve with age, especially when allowed to ripen in a tin box. When made without butter or egg yolk they last almost indefinitely and become rather like hardtack.

The keeping quality of gingerbread gave rise to a special role of this sweet, since particularly beautiful specimens were sometimes kept as an adornment for a wall or shelf. The most popular shape of all was the heart, which served the same purpose as an engagement ring in rural regions, where it was purchased by poor suitors who with this gift pledged their heart and hand when proposing marriage. Hence the sweetmaker's stall at the local fair was often the meeting point of young lovers. Even today, Christmas markets and bazaars still sell gingerbread hearts and figures, although they have lost some of their charm.

Gingerbread and lebkuchen recipes call for a small amount of leavening. Sometimes, for the sake of tradition, potash or hartshorn is used, without which some people swear these winter treats just don't taste "the way they used to." Whatever the leavening, gingerbread and lebkuchen lose some of their profile when baked. This loss is amply compensated for by the pretty white or colored icing which is then piped on to the baked goods. Hearts are often decorated with short poems or sweet sayings in attractive calligraphy.

Two types of dough are capable of rendering detail extremely well, especially when left to dry overnight before being baked in a slow oven. One is the *Springerle*, which originated in Southern Germany in the fifteenth century. It is a whisked egg cookie flavored with anise, once gaudily painted but nowadays left in its sophisticated natural ivory color. Its subject matter includes gentlefolk in ornate costumes, cavaliers on horseback, and hunting scenes—a residue of courtly life. The other is the *Tirggel*, a brittle, thin, rectangular, hexagonal, or round cookie from Zurich, made of flour and honey in the approximate proportion of three to one, with a little cinnamon and nutmeg thrown in. The decorative images evolved from fashionable courtly figures to those having an anecdotal or educational content, such as depictions of the William Tell saga, or celebrations of technical progress in the forms of bridges, railways, vehicles, and school buildings. During the nineteenth century *Tirggel* were used as objects of nascent tourism: those with cityscapes were shaped as postcards to be sold to out-of-town visitors, or to be sent overseas in special tin boxes.

Curiously, *Tirggel* used to be slang for drunkenness. It seems that the inebriated husband would try to soothe his irate wife with a package of these goodies following a bout of drinking at the local tavern. In the majority of cases he was forgiven, just as two thousand years earlier the household gods and other divinities were appeased by similar gestures.

GINGERBREAD COOKIES
Corncob: 6¼ x 2¼"; Slice of Pumpkin Pie: 3 x 5"; Pumpkin: 3½" diameter. Patty Paige, New York. Blue Barn:
4½" high; Tower: 7" high. Anonymous, New York

These cookies go on sale at Thanksgiving time. Ms. Paige's original designs and unusually colored icing have reinvigorated the gingerbread trade, which in recent time has become mostly a home craft. The creator of the blue-and-brown barn and the striped tower has taken a different approach; the dough has been tinted before being assembled and baked.

(OPPOSITE) GINGERBREAD HOUSE
10 x 7½ x 8½". United States

Gingerbread houses became the rage after the opening of Humperdinck's opera Hänsel und Gretel in 1893 and never went out of fashion. They are often fabricated at home with the participation of children. Homemade miniature cookies, marzipan fruit, store-bought candies and chocolates, icing, or silver dragées all qualify as decoration.

24

Cake

THE proverbial forty eggs which have to be beaten by hand with three pounds of sugar for an hour and a half to produce a cake worthy of a Victorian table indicate quite clearly that baking a cake was not an everyday affair, even in the nineteenth century, when sugar had, after hundreds of years, finally spread beyond society's upper classes. By then, its affordability was due to the discovery by the German chemist A. S. Marggraf that sucrose could be extracted from carrots and certain beets, which are temperate crops, while cane sugar had to be imported from the Tropics. Although this did not make big waves when revealed in 1747, half a century later Napoleon took up the idea during the continental blockade and encouraged the cultivation and industry of sugar beets, thus doing for the sweet powder what Henry IV had done for the poule-au-pot: he made it part of every French household.

While in our day sugar has become downright cheap—a pound of it costs less than a single bus fare—our puritanical attitudes about "indulging" in sweets and our obsession with health have insured the cake's role as a celebratory gesture. The pennies once carefully saved and put aside for costly ingredients have their modern equivalent in another currency. Today we are not counting the money spent but the number of calories eaten, and we have even been persuaded by the notion of an "allowance" to be judiciously spent on such things as a scoop of ice cream or a portion of pie à la mode.

Another commodity which has a new price attached to it is the element of time. Since fewer and fewer women have the leisure to bake cookies and cakes at home, the occasion for serving a cake has become a special one. Often it signals a

HEART WITH FLOWERS
12" diameter. Cheryl Kleinman, Brooklyn, New York

Hearts and roses, the most enduring of all symbols, apply to many occasions. This marzipan-covered chocolate cake is an offering to a Sweet Sixteen party, the American coming-of-age celebration for a young girl.

holiday, the celebration of an achievement, or one of life's milestones: birth, the coming of age, marriage, or even death. Today it may strike us as odd that death should have provided pastry makers with important commissions. But funerals in the past were among the grandest of occasions—European courts vied with each other in pomp, circumstance, and food displays, just as they did on the occasion of royal visits, political alliances, and princely feasts. And at the lower end of the social scale we find funeral biscuits and burial cakes; in Yorkshire, for example, one of the poorer districts of England, it was a customary part of the funeral rites to treat the mourners to cake and ale—sometimes at a ruinous cost to the family of the deceased.

The festive occasion for which the cake is the crowning moment dictates that a great deal of care and artistry go into its production. Seasonal motifs have remained the classical standbys of pastry chefs the world over. France's strong suit are the Bûche de Noel, followed by the Feast of the Epiphany's Galette des Rois, which is a round, flattish cake with a sunburst or grid design on the top layer, and a bean or small trinket hidden inside. It can also be a ring-shaped brioche, bejeweled with candied fruit and topped by a golden paper crown. The "Bûche," or Yule log, is known beyond the borders of France, owing its popularity to the effective way in which bark can be simulated by chocolate. Elsewhere the tree's mystic powers are glorified in the form of birch logs, pine cones, the German *Baumkuchen,* and cookies made to resemble oak leaves or wood shavings. Cakes in the shape of Easter lambs, snakes, and apples, which delight old and young alike, are other recurrent symbols woven into Christian context by way of the Old Testament.

On the whole, however, pastry making is less about symbolism than about architecture. According to the nineteenth-century luminary Carême, patisserie is one of the fine arts along with painting, sculpture, poetry, and music. Marie-Antoine Carême, who is the true father of French haute cuisine as we know it, gave his detailed knowledge and passionate attention to all its aspects, including pastry making. Among the many books he wrote, two in particular are worthy in this regard—*Le Patissier Royal Parisien* and *Le Patissier Pittoresque,* three octavo volumes with 169 plates all drawn by the author. Anyone who has ever tried to apply royal icing is acutely aware that without a deft hand it is not possible to do a halfway decent job. Thus, every patissier must have a pronounced artistic streak; penmanship is only one of the many required disciplines of this exacting profession. As for Carême, his authorship was not limited to culinary writing. He also wrote two books on architecture, one of which contained plans for buildings in St. Petersburg. This love of the fine arts set the tone for his pastries and edible centerpieces, which he designed in every conceivable variation. The great ruins of Athens, Turkish fountains, Indian pavilions, Venetian bridges, Chinese hermitages, Egyptian belvederes, and myriads more were built out of cake, nougat, caramel, sugar paste, marzipan, and any other sweet substance that would qualify as a building element for his romantic schemes.

Even the world of fiction offered fanciful creations. Emma Bovary's provincial wedding cake was ordered from a

YULELOG AND BIRCHLOG
Approx. 4½″ diameter, 10″ long. United States

The undisputed popularity of the Bûche de Noël as an affirmative seasonal symbol is such that many families believe Christmas is incomplete without it. Basically a simple jellyroll spruced up with a buttercream filling and an ornate, barklike, chocolate coat, it has a cousin in the birchlog, also of Northern origin and served at various occasions, including Easter.

PEACHES
3″ diameter. New York

TURKEY PLATTER
9½″ diameter. New York

Two genoise-type pastries, made by a Hungarian baker in New York City, conceal a chocolate mousse center and are covered in marzipan and glazed with fondant. The modern consumer would consider them a temptation similar to the apple in the Garden of Eden, for in our time a high caloric content has become synonymous with sin. Whether apples or peaches, fruit has long symbolized earthly desire and indulgence.

This turkey, fashioned out of sponge cake and marzipan, glazed with caramel, surrounded by marzipan vegetables, and set on a nougatine plate, is not a pop-art sculpture by Claes Oldenburg, but a cake offered for sale in New York City during Thanksgiving. This holiday, traditionally marked by a roast turkey and highlighted with nature's bounty, cuts across cultural lines.

(OPPOSITE) SERPENT
10″ diameter. Madrid

This glistening, baked marzipan cake, a traditional Spanish Christmas and New Year's confection, is filled with preserved fruit and decorated with icing; it weighs a full four pounds. The snake, a phallic as well as biblical image, is a recurrent motif in breads and sweets. Because of its real glass eyes, this particular one looks like a dragon from a fairy tale.

new patissier in Yvetot, who hand delivered this *pièce montée* himself:

> *The base of it was a square blue cardboard box in the form of a temple, adorned with porticoes and colonnades and little stucco statuettes all around in niches spangled with stars made of goldpaper foil. On the second tier was a turret of Savoy cake, surrounded by miniature fortifications in candied angelica, almonds, dried raisins, and orange sections. Finally, on the top layer there was a green meadow with rocks and lakes of jelly, with tiny boats made of hazelnut shells, and a small Cupid poised on a swing of chocolate, the posts of which terminated in real rosebuds.*

This little chef d'oeuvre executed in mixed media had all the entertainment value of its genre, in which appearance had an edge over taste and which had taken root many generations before.

Already during the Renaissance inspiration for edible table decorations was sought from the arts, and sculptors were sometimes called in to chisel allegorical or mythological figures out of large blocks of sugar. The appetite for visual entertainment at that time was tremendous. Banquets were far more than sumptuous meals: they were culinary spectacles of a magnificence we would find hard to reconstruct. The centerpieces gracing the large tables and sideboards were sugar sculptures and required the help not just of confectioners, but of all sorts of other artisans who were needed to provide the architectural plans, wooden scaffoldings, and tools and molds (sometimes made of silver!) needed for the constructions of these *pièces monteés*.

Savory food was also elaborately sculpted and decorated; roasted and re-feathered peacocks, for example, were commonplace. Kitchen artists neatly sewed together halved roasted piglets with roasted birds, thus startling and amazing diners with fantastic bestial creations. Fanciful heraldic animals were assembled by pastry chefs and family crests were reproduced in aspic. Musicians, jugglers, and jesters were a necessity at such fêtes, and sometimes made their appearance by jumping out of an enormous baked pie.

The pastry chef was responsible for pies, tarts, pâtés, and certain jellied dishes which were poured to set in metal or ceramic molds. Pie crusts in the shape of lions or rams served as baked containers and were filled with fish or meat mixtures just before serving. Only rarely did they hold fruit. There was no clear distinction between sweet and salty courses, since sugar was indiscriminately used on nearly everything from fish to fowl. Although the pie had not changed substantially since the Middle Ages, cakes only made their appearance around 1600, largely owing to the fact that most kitchens lacked built-in ovens and had to make do with portable contraptions on trivets and pots heated from above with hot embers. The first collection of pastry and egg recipes was published in 1654, probably by La Varenne. This book was a milestone in culinary history inasmuch as it contained definitions of weights and measures, which were usually absent from early cookery books—a fact which has cast

ARMCHAIR
Cake: 8½″, sugar carpet: 11½ x 15″. Colette Peters, New York

Peters, a former designer for Tiffany's, invents, bakes, and decorates cakes for every occasion. She created this lounge chair for a party celebrating someone's retirement. Inside is the darkest of chocolate cakes. The slipcover is done in rolled fondant, a paste made of sugar, gelatine, glucose, and glycerine, which has a certain elasticity and stays soft for a day or two.

a permanent veil over much food of the past.

The three-dimensional character of the cake is largely dependent on its ingredients. Beaten eggs produce the air that makes the cake rise; sugar adds the staying power. Height commands attention, and vertical shapes denote festivity. This holds true for food too: it is easier to elicit cries of delight with pyramids than with pancakes. An interesting link is formed by the brioche, which is made of flour, butter, eggs, yeast, and some salt and sugar. A ball of dough resting on a fluted, lower loaf is meant to lend it upward mobility. The finished product is more than a bread and not yet a cake—the architecture is there, but the decoration is missing. In defense of Marie Antoinette it must be said that when she suggested that the poor should eat cake, she really only meant brioche.

The true soul of the cake is in its decoration. The sight of a simple dusting of confectioners' sugar on a homemade cake is enough to warm the cockles of one's heart. It is the humblest of decorations, representative of one of the most basic family rituals: the sharing of a pleasurable moment. The means and methods at the disposal of the professional patissier to embellish or disguise a multilayered cake, on the other hand, are nearly unlimited, and the many years of his apprenticeship are a must to equip him with the necessary skills to give free reign to his imagination and to achieve practically any desired effect.

He is the keeper of apricot glazes, buttercreams, frostings, fillings, fondants, meringue, almond paste, chocolate ganache, royal icing, crystallized flowers, nougatine, and silver-coated dragees, also known as sugar balls. Among dozens of attractive implements are such tools as crimpers, spatulas, decorating combs, paint brushes, and above all, a pastry bag with 105 different nozzles. With these the patissier pipes trellises, festoons, garlands, swags, and basket weave patterns on multi-tiered layer cakes; he paints chocolate silhouettes, calligraphs Gothic letters and Art Deco numbers, applies garret frills, clusters of grapes and flowers, and draws his inspiration anywhere from the Rococo vocabulary

of the classical confectioner to contemporary Pop art images. In short, he delves into the varied techniques that make the patissier's profession the most decorative of the gastronomic arts.

Of course the most glorious of all cakes is the wedding cake, the flagship of the confectioner's craft. While the extravagant sugar sculptures that were once flaunted by the European nobility are no longer produced, their offspring, the wedding cake, is experiencing a true revival. Contemporary versions are being created not only by chefs and patissiers but often, especially in the United States, by artistic women, who started making cakes as a cottage industry and ended up with a prestigious business, catering their elegant productions to a fashionable and demanding clientele. Whether educated at art school, trained as chefs, or self-taught, they each have a recognizable style of their own, and the young brides can choose between many different possibilities—often to the amazement of their mothers, for whom, earlier in this century, a wedding cake was something of a standard item, pale inside and out. It has been said that at a modern American wedding the three most important things are the bride, her dress, and the cake. The groom, alas, is further down on the list.

The physical appearance of the wedding cake varies as markedly from country to country as do the traditions and habits connected with it, providing an interesting facet of culinary anthropology. The French pièce de résistance at christenings, first communions, and weddings alike is the *croquembouche,* that tall, sparkling, cone-shaped assembly of caramelized cream puffs, which recalls the pastry chefs' earliest efforts to achieve height. It is here that we can best visualize the now defunct custom of the bride and groom kissing each other over a pile of sweet buns. The Italian *torta di nozze* looks very different and reminds one of Italy's Renaissance sugar architecture. The *torta di nozze* is a multi-tiered construction of flat, white, round cakes in graduating

LAMB
10" high, base 8 x 11". Cheryl Kleinman, Brooklyn, New York

The lamb is a traditional Easter cake which 30 years ago was sold by Schrafft's in New York. This particular one, covered in fondant and adorned with marzipan, was made from a commercially available aluminum mold. As a symbol, this animal has had an extensive career, being the offspring of the biblical and Middle Eastern sacrificial lamb.

MOTHER'S DAY CAKE
10" diameter. New York

Mother's Day is traditionally linked to flowers. This cake was ordered from the New York Exchange for Women's Work, that venerable institution established in 1878 through which women sell their homemade goods to get some extra income, be it from cookies or handknits. Bake sales and bazaars at which special sweets are sold have been a time-honored way to raise money for charitable causes.

WEDDING CAKE
14″ high; bottom tier: 10″ diameter. Kevin Pavlina, Detroit

The chef displays an haute couturier's flair for coordinating the looks of the wedding cake with the dress of the bride. Ribbons made of pastillage are draped over a two-tiered cake and accentuated by sensuous roses made of the same fragile material, which becomes brittle when dry.

WEDDING CAKE
Approx. 15″ high; bottom tier: 14″ diameter. Joseph Gilmartin and Rebecca Russel, Patisserie Lanciani, New York

The current passion for white chocolate is indulged in this wedding cake. Broad bands of white chocolate—harder to work with than dark—are elegantly folded over the top of the three tiers in a wavelike manner. Tiny flowers and berries made of sugar grace the sides.

(OPPOSITE) OCTAGONAL BOX
5″ high, approx. Base: 12″ diameter. Kevin Pavlina, Detroit

This unusual edible centerpiece was created by an accomplished pastry chef from Michigan. A round cake for twelve people is housed in a pagodalike octagonal framework assembled from flat pieces of royal icing, a style known among confectioners as English Nirvana. It is a complex piece of craftsmanship that requires mastery of such techniques as beadwork and run-in icing to achieve the quilted effect on the surface, which pleasantly offsets the rigidity of the structure.

sizes, each separated by tall columns and ornamented with white icing and sugar roses. According to Waverly Root, it was Catherine de Medici who brought the first three-tiered cake to France, where she arrived in 1533 as the bride of the future Henri II. Though she did not revolutionize French gastronomy as is often claimed, she nevertheless must be given full credit for the many pastries and sweetmeats she introduced from Italy. These were genuinely novel imports to France, as were, surprisingly, the art of brandy-making and fruit-flavored liqueurs, with which Italians still flavor their cakes more liberally than other nations.

The British wedding cake is yet another thing. Moreover, its history is available to us, for Britain's food history is particularly well documented and analyzed, perhaps attributable to her natives' scholarly bent and gift of the gab rather than to the lushness of English food. Normally, the English wedding cake—originally called bride-cake—is a three-tiered stack, covered with white icing and deliriously piped-on ornamentation, crowned by flowers or a figurative ornament. The inside is a rich fruitcake. For those relatives or friends who are unable to attend the wedding it is customary to send a slice of the cake. Sometimes, the top layer of this cake was set aside for future purposes such as the christening of the first child, when it was re-iced for the occasion. This suggests a cake with a considerable shelf life, a highly pregnant bride, or else a freezer, none of which would do for a *croquembouche,* which goes soggy before the day is over.

It is of course impossible to talk about British family affairs without bringing in Queen Victoria, whose influence is still apparent at many English celebrations. Her own wedding cake was a simple round cake, nevertheless weighing three hundred pounds. By the time her children married, wedding fashion had taken on a new direction. The new cakes were up to seven feet high and incredibly elaborate, decorated with portraits of the Royal family made in sugar, among many other complicated embellishments. Also new was the idea of having these cakes photographed and published in illustrated magazines around the country. This awareness of public relations has remained one of the cornerstones of the British Monarchy. Queen Victoria was furthermore an astute observer of people's habits and tried out her future dinner guests at teatime, when she would watch how much sugar everyone used. Those who amply helped themselves were considered all right and free of the suspicion of being alcoholics.

That women, in the past at least, favored sugar over alcohol, may well be one of the reasons why we tend to associate them with cake more than we do men, both as consumers and producers. Baking has always been the stonghold of the so-called weaker sex, and cookbooks addressed themselves early on to the "gentle ladies." While male pastry chefs have traditionally occupied the prestigious professional posts, women have always had a finger in the pie, so to speak. Or, as we read in the introduction of *The Dessert Book* by "A Boston Lady," published in 1872: "While the preparation of soups, joints, and gravies is left to ruder and stronger hands, the delicate fingers of the lady of the household are best fitted to mingle the proportions of exquisite desserts."

WEDDING CAKE
25" high; bottom tier: 16" diameter. Sylvia Weinstock, New York

This wedding cake for 200 guests was designed and made by the grande dame of pastillage flowers. The roses, irises, poppies, pansies, lilies, tulips, and other blossoms are based on a close study of nature. These delicious-tasting, fragile sugar flowers are hand-sculpted petal by petal and applied at the last moment to the freshest of cakes.

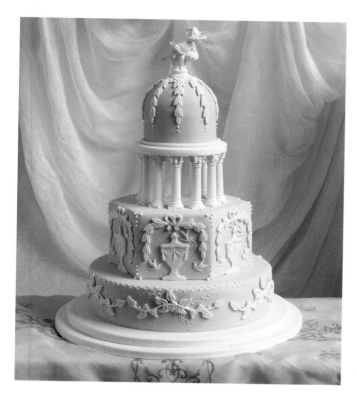

WEDDING CAKE
28″ high including angel; bottom tier: 16″ diameter.
Cheryl Kleinman, Brooklyn, New York

A three-tiered architectural wedding cake is built in the shape of a classical rotunda and covered in rolled fondant, the pale color of which subtly conveys the orange flavor of the cake inside. Its decoration was chosen from books and illustrations, and special molds were ordered for its execution.

(OPPOSITE) WEDDING CAKE
27″ high; base: 24 x 24″. Cile Bellefleur-Burbridge, Danvers, Massachusetts

An enchanting garden pavilion bedecked with elaborate floral detail is the dazzling accomplishment of a pastry chef well known for her classical approach to wedding cakes. The all-white decoration is made of traditional royal icing. Some parts, such as the trellises, are first piped onto a flat surface; when dry, they are positioned on the cake. Other details, such as the garlands and clusters of grapes, are piped onto the cake itself.

WEDDING CAKE
20″ high; bottom tier: 17″ diameter. Palmer Butterfield,
South Glastonbury, Connecticut

This four-tiered tribute to Wedgwood jasperware is a cake decorator's virtuoso act achieved in buttercream piped directly onto the cake. The only tools used were a spatula and pastry bag with a few different nozzles. In the 18th century porcelain took over from sugar sculpture; today, the opposite trend has set in: edible decoration simulates porcelain.

Marzipan

MARZIPAN is a paste made of ground almonds, fine sugar, a little egg white, and a few drops of rosewater. Some people have a passion for this Old World treat, while others shudder at the thought of its intense sweetness. Nobody, however, questions its excellence as a decorative material. The proportion of almond to sugar in marzipan varies according to its use, for apart from being eaten in its pure state it also has numerous applications as fillings, centers, garnishes, or coverings for cakes and petit fours. The best-tasting kind has a higher almond content, while augmenting the quantity of powdered sugar stiffens the paste and makes it more malleable. Its smooth texture allows it to be formed freehand into any size or shape, and unlike many of the confectioner's other basic materials, it can be worked without haste. Its unequaled property as a modeling material has spawned many artifacts such as fruits, figures, animals, and small objects. As these only have to harden and do not require baking, once formed they retain their shape perfectly. Color can be kneaded into the paste or painted on afterward, and a special edible lacquer is apt to add that touch of realism that is the hallmark of this unique confection.

Much ink has flowed about the origin of the word marzipan. The earlier theory that it is based on *panis Marcis*, Saint Mark's bread, has been dropped in favor of the explanation that the Byzantine coin *mauthaban* came to Venice as *matabam* and stood for a cubic measure, which in thirteenth-century Naples, Sicily, and Provence became synonymous with a small box. These wooden boxes, which figure prominently in old still-life paintings, served as containers for sweets, and

TURNIP, MOREL, ZUCCHINI, LEEK, CABBAGE, BOLETUS
1¾–4½". Switzerland

Marzipan vegetables like these are sold in Geneva at the time of the Escalade, *a holiday in December that commemorates the courageous* Mère Royaume, *who successfully defended the town against an attack by the Savoyards by pouring boiling soup over the intruders.*

42

so it is believed that the name of the wooden container eventually was transferred to its content, marzipan, or marchpane.

This convoluted etymological development stands in remarkable contrast to the substance itself, which, given its simple recipe, has hardly changed in some nine hundred years. Marzipan is one of the few foods which must taste pretty much the same today as it did when the Crusaders came home from their arduous journeys abroad, regaling their wives and children with such exotic souvenirs as marzipan and spices. While this scenario is a romantic version of what may have happened, during the first four hundred years of this millennium when the Crusaders returned to Northwestern Europe, they certainly popularized many new ingredients and changed forever Europe's epicurean knowledge and desires.

There can be no doubt that marzipan originated in the Arab world. Almonds, frequently mentioned in the Bible, were among the earliest cultivated food plants and grew in Anatolia, Greece, and throughout the Middle East. The Moors, who particularly liked citrus and almond trees, planted almond groves wherever they went; during the Islamic Expansion they were especially successful in Portugal and Spain, where conditions were ideal for these exacting nut-bearing trees.

Sugarcane too originated in the East, where it was known since antiquity. Its exact place of birth is disputed, but it probably came from India, where it was spotted by Nearchus, an officer in Alexander the Great's army, who described the tall grass as a reed which makes honey without the help of bees. In any case, its name derives from the Sanskrit *Sarkara*, for pebble or gravel, and for some time the crystals obtained from the sap of the stout plant were known as "Indian Salt." The cultivation of sugarcane and the technique of sugar production slowly spread westward over a period of more than fifteen hundred years, first to Persia (6th century A.D.), then to Syria and Africa, and later still to Crete, southern Spain, and Sicily. From 1300 onward, sugar from the Middle East began to appear in Europe. But it was rare, fairly unrefined, reached its destination slowly, and was costly to transport. Thus its place was on the apothecary's shelf, where it was sold as medicine in minute quantities, as were marzipan and spices. The apothecary put it to advantage in his dispensary to disguise his bitter concoctions, and made so-called confections (from the Latin *conficere*, to put together), which, apart from herbal mixtures, sometimes contained such rarities as gold dust and ground pearls.

Initially, apothecaries everywhere were supplied by the Italians, or more precisely by the Venetians, who were the first to build up the sugar industry, setting up refineries for the expensive commodity which was bought in crude form from the Middle East. Part of Venice's fortune was made by keeping the European nobility in refined sugar. The international upper crust had developed such an uncommon liking for the expensive white stuff that several conscientious sixteenth-century physicians felt obliged to criticize the fact that sugar and marzipan were gaining ground for "banqueting purposes" rather than as medicine. They were gifts worthy of kings, popes, and emperors, and along with spices became the insignia of conspicuous wealth. Despite their exorbitant price, sugar and marzipan were used in such excess that luxury laws had to be made to keep their consumption within bounds. Meanwhile, many Italians became proficient confectioners and prospered accordingly. The first book on the confectioner's art was published in Venice in 1541 and translated into French the same year under the name of *Bastiment de Recettes*. Instructions included those for preserving fruit, making jams, candied orange peel, quince paste, and nougat. Some, if not most, of these techniques, like the making of marzipan, had been picked up by the Italians from their business partners in the Arab world.

Like lebkuchen and gingerbread, marzipan became a regional specialty and a Christmas treat, particularly in the North, often named after the cities which produced it, like Odense in Denmark, or Lübeck in Germany, both of which were ports re-

FOOD PLATTERS
Oval platter: 5½" long. Switzerland

These miniature marzipan plates, pan, and platters complete with sausages, pork chops, steak, noodles, and an assortment of cheeses are meant for the doll house. Beyond that, they are strangely reminiscent of burial objects and of medieval illusion foods, which were served between courses at banquets to entertain the guests.

45

POMEGRANATE, MEDLARS, FIGS, PEARS,
CACTUS PEARS, CHERRIES, ROASTED
CHESTNUTS, SALAMI, AND SALAMI
SANDWICH
Pomegranate: 3" diameter; chestnut: 1½". Sicily

*The most exquisite of marzipan sculptures come
from Sicily, where the love for rituals, traditions,
and sweets runs deep. The pomegranate, figs,
cherries, pears, and roasted chestnuts above are all
life-size. Now manufactured by confectioners at
large and throughout the year, lush symbols of
abundance such as these remind us that Sicily still
holds a celebration in spring for Demeter, the
Greek goddess of agriculture and fruitfulness.*

ceiving valuable almond and sugar shipments from Mediterranean trading posts. Lübeck, once the leader of the Hanseatic League, is the home of the famous firm J. G. Niederegger, and has a well-documented and continuous marzipan history dating back to 1300. Königsberger marzipan, another German classic, is worth mentioning as a variation on the theme: its traditional bite-sized hearts are embellished with candied cherries and angelica and are baked until their notched edges take on a brown tint. Originally, marzipan was almost always baked.

In the South, Toledo in Spain and Portogao in Portugal are renowned for their marzipan, and they must have been among the first Europeans to produce it from homegrown raw materials, as sugarcane was acclimated in Spain, on the Canary Islands, and on Madeira around 1400. Similarly, Aix-en-Provence in France makes the intriguing calisson d'Aix, a pâte d'amandes on a wafer base, containing ground-up bits of candied melon rind and orange peel, which relates it to the sweetmeats of the earliest cookery books. Moreover, calissons d'Aix have retained the lozenge shape in which the apothecary formerly offered this marzipan sweet as medicine.

In German-speaking countries the apothecaries held on to the lucrative privilege of selling sugar and producing their healthful confections for as long as they could; sometimes they even published their medico-culinary insights and recipes. But around 1800, after several hundred years and, as one can imagine, after heated battles, they lost the spice trade to the grocerers and sugar craft to the confectioners. Every country developed its own specialty professions, and its own guild rules and regulations, which drew strict lines between the various spheres of activites. In Germany and Austria, the confectioner was a skilled artist capable of hand-modeling marzipan figures and doing elaborate icing; but he was not allowed to handle flour if he was not classifed as a fancy baker. Further evidence of the former connection between medicine and food is supported by the fact that today many old cookery books are an adjunct of medical libraries.

To the nimble-fingered kitchen artists of the fourteenth to the sixteenth centuries, marzipan was not just a fine food but a welcome sculpting material, which could be modeled like clay. So could its sister material, sugar paste or pastillage, a similarly pliable but less flavorful dough, made with the help of tragacanth. Tragacanth, another of the pharmacists' wares, is a powder extracted from the juice of a gum plant which has neither a distinct taste, odor, or color, and is completely harmless. It does, however, add body to various materials and in the past was used by pastry cooks, bookbinders, perfumers, and lacemakers alike. Thus the main use of marzipan and sugar paste (the two were often mixed) became foremost a decorative one, and the historical significance of marzipan is to be found as much in its function as in its taste.

During the late Middle Ages and the Renaissance, wealth was flaunted at all the European courts in the form of showy sugar and marzipan sculptures, brilliantly colored with dyes obtained from saffron, sandalwood, roses, heliotrope, mint, parsley, violets, and blood. Gold was applied whenever possible, that is to say when sumptuary laws did not impose restrictions. These decorations served as the culminating events at banquets and court functions; consumption was of secondary importance. Allegorical pageants modeled in tragacanth and sugar originated in Italy under the name of *trionfi di tavola* or *macchine di zucchero figurate* and were reported from many festivities. In Ferrara, the week-long wedding of Isabella d'Este and Francesco Gonzaga in 1490 was described as a sequence of lavish sugar displays for days on end. Modena, Padua, and Florence did not lag far behind with representations of castles, animals, and ships, and were outdone only by the Turks, who in 1580 created a forty-two-foot-long sugar zoo consisting of nine elephants, seventeen lions, nineteen leopards, giraffes, storks, and cranes—all of it carried around by a contingent of strong men. These gigantic sugar representations, also including battlefields, chariots, nymphs, and mythological *tableaux vivants* were somewhat incongruously called "subtleties." Pageboys paraded them about or set them on platforms nearby, where the ladies could amuse themselves after dinner bombarding the sweet-filled sceneries with sugarplums.

While the above "subtleties" were reserved for the grander occasions, every ordinary banquet had an equally amusing sideline, the so-called puzzle courses or illusion foods, served in between regular courses and therefore called entremets. The idea of these surprise dishes was that they should tickle the fancy of the diner by deceiving and fooling him. Trompe l'oeil was the main objective: they had to look like one kind of food but turn out to be something different. The more outlandish and exuberant the effect, the bigger the applause. Despite the emphasis on appearance, these dishes were meant for consumption. Delicate flowers of sugar belong into this category, or hams and sausages made of marzipan, mock entrails of prunes and nuts, plates and glasses which could be eaten, golden apples made from meat—the lists were endless and every cookbook had suggestions for the wealthy housewife on how to go about to fool and delight her guests. In 1609 the English cookbook author Sir Hugh Plats instructed his reader of *Delights for Ladies* on how to model marzipan and come up with "conceits" for festive purposes. Not only did he think on a large scale, including among his ideas gardens, animals, buildings, and allegorical figures, but Sir Hugh attended to the details as well, listing buttons, beetles, charms, snakes, snails, frogs, roses, chives, shoes, slippers, keys, knives, gloves, letters, knots, or any other "lumball."

Current marzipan production still has a trompe-l'oeil quality or vaguely gimmicky aspect. Sicilian fruit and vegetable sculptures are executed approaching nature with astounding similarity by including realistic defects like blemishes and bruises. A great many curious animals find their way to fancy shops too, from the traditional good-luck piglets to storks,

mice, and crocodiles. Needless to say, children take the same pleasure in the surprise element of edible fakes as did adults in earlier days. Tackling and eating these pieces is usually done with much gusto and accompanied by peals of laughter. As an anthropological footnote it should be mentioned that when it comes to the eating of marzipan or chocolate creatures, the head always goes first, be it of friend or foe. Larger artifacts such as dollhouse-type stage sets or still-life compositions not meant for the palate continue to be created by professional confectioners for entries in tradeshows and prize-winning competitions, or as eye-catching window displays.

If marzipan is on something of a decline today it is because other materials have taken over its decorative function. Toward the end of the eighteenth century porcelain began to displace sugar sculpture. It was finer, more durable, pretty, colorful, and unlike marzipan, impervious to humidity and climate. In short, it was more modern. The miniature landscapes, mythological sceneries, shepherdesses, and garden paraphernalia which previously were made of marzipan became imagery favored by porcelain manufacturers. But as time never stands still, we have already moved on to another round of improvements. The bride-and-groom figurines on top of many wedding cakes are no longer made of sugar, or marzipan, or porcelain, nor are the columns supporting the cake tiers: plastic as a lightweight and labor-saving ornament has come to the aid of the confectioner. But this is not where our story ends. In Japan, which excels at imitation in general and at imitation food in particular, the entire wedding cake is made of plastic. It is for rent to those of its citizens who embrace Western culture but cannot afford the real thing. For the cake-cutting ritual, which is of course part of the ceremony, a slot is provided in a suitable spot. Is it possible that on some future day we will look back nostalgically and remember plastic as an endearingly old-fashioned and therefore cherished material?

STORK
5" high, Zurich

Marzipan storks have been around for generations and were of great help to mothers in pre-sex-education days when the arrival of a new baby had to be explained. This stork has legs made from matches and is surrounded by candy pebbles.

MICE
2½" long, Paris

These marzipan confections for children allude to the fact that the Parisians occasionally ate rats during periods of famine.

TROUT
6″ long. Annecy, France

Marzipan fish are popular throughout the year. In previous centuries they were often used as decorative elements during Lent. Even in the Arab world, the shape was known: it is recorded that the 10th-century poet Al Mutanabbi received a marzipan fish immersed in honey as a token of appreciation for a particularly successful poem.

SHRIMP
2″ long. South of France

France with its haute cuisine never veers far from realistic representation when it comes to sweets. These life-size marzipan shrimp are displayed on a tray half-filled with candy pebbles, also made in France.

APRICOTS, PLUMS, PEARS, AND APPLES
Average size ³/₄″. Switzerland

A yearly onion market is one of the harvest festivals held in Bern, Switzerland's capital, where farmers' wives gather to sell their beautiful onion braids on the last Monday in November. Tiny baskets of miniature marzipan fruit, such as the above, are sold there in confectionery shops for the children, who are unlikely to appreciate the onions.

THREE MONKEYS
2″ high

The provenance and purpose of these "Hear no evil, see no evil, speak no evil" monkeys are undocumented, but they clearly demonstrate the versatility of marzipan in creating such unique imitations. Plastic molds can be made of any artifact, which was probably the case for the specimens above.

DANCER'S LEGS
5″ long. Switzerland

No comment seems necessary.

FEMALE LEGS
4½″ long. Switzerland

With this second, different pair of marzipan legs, the suspicion arises that maybe there is more to these limbs than meets the eye. In Calabria, for instance, spiced breads are made in the shape of human limbs for the feast of San Rocco, when these ex-votos are offered to the saint.

PIGS AND PIGLETS
1¼–3″. Germany and Denmark

Marzipan pigs and piglets are good-luck items from Germany and Denmark, usually linked to New Year's Day.

Ice Cream

IN OUR otherwise well-documented history of civilization, the recording of culinary taste and its evolution has been done rather casually, if not incidentally. Much of it is based on old cookery books, which are an unreliable source as far as dates are concerned, since recipes were often written down generations after they were invented. Another drawback of food history is a persistent and widespread tendency toward plagiarism or substantial "borrowing" among cookbook authors. Thus, in the genesis of that divine but elusive substance, ice cream, it is nearly impossible to put one's finger with surety on a specific place of origin or date.

The accounts as to where ice cream or frozen desserts first appeared differ widely. China, India, Persia, and Arabia are among the geographical origins cited, and Alexander the Great and the great itinerant Marco Polo are also invoked. Emperor Nero (54 A.D.–68 A.D.) had Alpine snow relayed by runners, which he then flavored with fruit pulp and honey. Moghul rulers in India acted similarly, using snow from the Himalayas, whereas Montezuma enjoyed his snow confection with chocolate syrup. During a truce, the story goes that Saladin, the Arab sultan, treated Richard the Lionhearted to his first sherbet made from the snows of the Lebanon mountain range. And nearly two hundred and fifty years later, back on England's shores at Henry V's coronation, the English noblemen got to taste something called "*crem frez.*" Catherine de Medici is automatically invoked when it comes to gastronomic debates, but whether or not she knew about ice cream is frankly open to conjecture.

It is with the name of the Sicilian Francesco Procopio dei Coltelli, a guild

ICE CREAM PYRAMID
7" high; base: 9". St. Ambroeus, New York

Pyramids of ice cream fruits are among the great classical desserts that graced the sumptuous tables of Louis XIV. Today, they are the specialty of the Milanese firm St. Ambroeus, which caters these and similar ice cream sculptures to its New York clientele. The flavor of the ice cream usually corresponds to the fruit it represents. A nougatine tray forms the base.

member of the limonadiers and distillateurs of Paris, that the reputation of ice cream begins to solidify, as here it is not just connected with a name but with an address. Signor Procopio opened a café in Paris around 1670 in the Rue des Fossés-Saint-Germain-des-Prés (now the Rue de l'Ancienne Comédie, and still the site of Restaurant Procope), where he sold various ice creams and water ices as great novelties in a stylish interior decked out with chandeliers and marble-topped tables, apparently inspired by the Caffé Florian on the Piazza San Marco in Venice (which also still exists). Signor Procopio's establishment was such a success that others sprang up from the Parisian pavement like mushrooms, especially on what was to become the Boulevard des Italiens, made fashionable by its cafés and their proprietors, with names like Café Napolitain, Frascati, Pratti, Tortoni. (Tortoni, incidentally, is also the name of a concoction of ice cream, rum, and macaroons still available in New York.)

Since ice cream was seldom prepared at home, the premises where it was offered quickly gained popularity and became notable for their decorations, which were characteristic of the genre. One hundred and fifty years after Procopio, a similar development took place on a different continent, when the American soda fountain was invented. Originally the words *soda fountain* referred to the actual apparatus that dispensed carbonated water, which in time became more ornate in decoration; soon, however, the soda fountain came to be the shop itself—a fancy interior full of elegant trappings, mirrors, glass umbrella lampshades, and housing a freestanding marble or alabaster counter equipped with an array of draught arms and syrup pumps. Across the country, these ice cream parlors were greatly helped onto their feet by Prohibition, and by 1920 thousands of these shrines for the enjoyment of frozen delights and nonalcoholic drinks had been built. Often, they became the social centers previously found in saloons and bars.

Turning the clock back to the early 1800s, Vienna was the town where ice cream was served year-round day and night. The liveliness of Vienna's intellectual and social life is best illustrated by the fact that toward the end of the eighteenth century the city had no fewer than eighty-three coffeehouses—all of which catered their special coffees and ice creams to men only. When ladies were to be entertained they were taken to the *Limonadehütten* and *Erfrischungszelte* (types of refreshment booths and tents), where ice cream and a multitude of cool exotic drinks could be had, such as almond or pistachio milk, fruit nectars, hypocras (a sugared wine), or rosoglio, a slightly alcoholic drink spiced with nutmeg, carnation, and anise. The goings-on in these locations were of such an effervescent gaiety that half of Vienna's population was believed to owe its existence to the seductive effects of these fun-loving places.

As the capital of the Austrian empire, Vienna had frequent contact with the Ottoman Turks, who were known for their predilection for things sweet and fragrant. The Turks were responsible for introducing Europe to tulips, lilacs, hyacinths, and last but not least, the kiosk, a structure first welcomed in the West as a garden ornament but later adapted as the pretty stand where refreshing drinks, ices, and newspapers could be obtained, often in pleasurable and parklike surroundings. Sherbet (from the Arab *charbet*) was a Turkish contribution to upper-class tables, although it never really caught on among the general population. Ice cream, on the other hand, was consumed copiously by all, often in Oriental flavors such as violet, rose, jasmine, orange flower, cinnamon, tea, and pomegranate.

By and large, though, it was the French who worked themselves to the forefront of the confectioner's profession. One of their first moves had been to introduce the *office,* an auxiliary cool kitchen, where preserving and confectionery could be handled away from the heat and impurities of fire and smoke. The manufacturing of frozen desserts benefitted from an even colder room in which straw-lined barrels and pewter *sarbotières* (sorbetières) were kept. These were cylindrical pewter containers which could be filled with the concoction to be frozen and could then be set within barrels packed with salt, ice, and saltpeter. To prevent the formation of large ice crystals during the freezing process, the sorbetière could be shaken or swiveled by its handle. It was in the eighteenth century that eggs and cream were added to the basic ice cream mixture, thus allowing for a more moldable sweet. La Chapelle, who addresses himself in his *Le Cuisinier Modern* (1733) to professional cooks, mentions a variety of cream- and custard-based ices, as well as coffee and chocolate flavors. He recommended such shapes as melon molds and Turk's head, also known as *Kugelhopf* in German.

By the time Diderot had our world catalogued in the eighteenth century, patissier, confiseur, and glacier had evolved into separate occupations, each with their special premises, sets of tools, and, significantly for readers of Diderot, specific illustrations in his great French *Encyclopédie.* For example, the glacier's decorative pewter molds are shown—fish, crayfish, fruits, and an asparagus stalk are all included—, clearly indicating that ice cream was a genteel food given to ornamentation. Whether called ice cream, cream ice, fruit ice, glacé, sherbet, sorbet, *fromage glacé* (not a cheese but a frozen cream concoction), gelato or semifreddo, the basic sweet mixture admirably lent itself to being frozen into an upright shape, and ice cream was indeed brought to new decorative heights. The vertical accents considered so desirable on Baroque tables found a new incarnation as ice cream sculptures, especially in the form of gaily colored *bombes glacées,* which have dominated festive menus ever since, or as jewel-like pyramids composed of smaller iced objects tinted in pastel hues.

That frozen cream was universally liked can be gleaned from the fact that even England, with its cool, damp climate, devised its own variety early, when ice was difficult to come by. Once the building of ice houses became fashionable several women became involved in the production of ice cream, headed by Mrs. Hannah Glasse (1708–1770) of "first-you-catch-your-hare-fame." Mrs. Glasse is frequently quoted for her all too vague ice cream recipe, although in fact hers was predated by Mrs. Mary Eales's, confectioner to her late Majesty Queen Anne, published in 1718. What Mrs. Glasse deserves to be praised for is that she was the first full-fledged female cookbook author in a field hitherto occupied by men. Thanks to her initiative and originality, a sizable list of women writers followed in her path, including Martha Bradley, *The British Housewife;* Mary Smith, *The Complete Housekeeper and Professed Cook;* and Charlotte and Sarah Mason, *The Lady's Assistant.* Each of the books by these women contained instructions for making ice cream. Outstanding among the cookbook writers were Mrs. Elizabeth Raffald (*The Experienced English Housekeeper,* 1769), who was the queen of wedding cakes, and a few generations later, Mrs. Agnes B. Marshall, who published her *Book of Ices* in 1885. Mrs. A. B. Marshall was not only a successful author—her general cookbook sold 60,000 copies—but an astute businesswoman with diverse entrepreneurial instincts. Mrs. Marshall ran several businesses simultaneously, which all benefitted from and cross-pollinated each other: a cooking school and employment agency for upper-class domestics in London in the 1880s, classroom demonstrations and lecture tours (one of them in the U.S.), the publication of a penny paper, and the selling of an extensive range of kitchen appliances, including her patented ice cream freezer, ice caves (cooling cabinets), and more than a thousand pretty ice cream molds. She marketed some edible products too, which came in bottles and containers that had her name pressed into the glass or em-

bossed into the tin. This was a far cry indeed from the modest Nancy Johnson, an American who in 1846 had invented the hand-cranked ice cream freezer and forgot, neglected, or decided not to patent this contraption, which soon became the highlight of many a summer afternoon and a symbol of American family life.

No chapter on ice cream would be complete without mentioning American ice cream lore, which is the most entertaining of them all, and indeed should be so at a per capita consumption of more than five gallons in a good year. Typically, the first sign of American ice cream was not a recipe in a cookery book but an advertisement in the *New York Gazette* on May 12, 1777, and another one in the *New York Post Boy* in 1786, when ice cream was still considered a rarity. Once blocks of ice became a transportable and saleable commodity—some of them came from Walden Pond outside Concord, Massachusetts—ice cream gained momentum rapidly. By 1850 it was hugely popular and widely available, thanks to street vendors and the genius of Nancy Johnson. Its meteoric rise from a delicacy to an everyday food was caused by the initial insight that ice cream was an

ideal way to deal with surplus milk, and by a steady stream of technical and mechanical inventions, from steam to electrical power, homogenizers, mechanical refrigeration, and new insulation concepts. Thus America rightfully enjoyed the reputation of being the land of milk and honey. And when in 1921 the new immigrants at Ellis Island were treated to their first American meal it featured a dish of ice cream, which many of them had never seen before, and they spread it on their bread with a knife.

Molded ice cream fancies were less important in America, though they were occasionally fabricated too, especially in the Phildalephia area, which was considered the ice cream capital of the United States in the late 1800s. On the whole, though, ice cream cones and Good Humor bars—each dating to the early years of this century—were far more manageable shapes than birds and flowers. Indeed, a case is to be made for ice cream tasting its best when licked straight from a cone without the concommitant crudity and adulterating experience of harsh utensils, allowing us to concentrate on nothing but the cool sensuality of its velvety texture and the blissful sensation of its sweet taste.

FLOWER BASKET
Approx. 6″ high. Confiserie R. Sprüngli, Zurich

Flowers, the symbols of spring, beauty, and transitoriness adorning a basket, are rendered in ice cream, a substance even more ephemeral than the flowers themselves. These frozen sculptures are assembled from separate pieces, made in different flavors, and then frozen in 19th-century pewter molds. Finishing touches applied with an airbrush device and piped-on whipped cream complete this exquisite but short-lived dream.

MAX AND MORITZ
Approx. 8″ high. Confiserie R. Sprüngli, Zurich

This ice cream sculpture, the crowning glory of any child's birthday party, depicts the cartoon characters known in America as the Katzenjammer Kids. These all-time favorite pranksters are the creation of satirist Wilhelm Busch (1832–1908) and loom large in every German-speaking childhood. Sprüngli's magnificent collection of ice cream molds dates from the turn of the century and also includes fairy-tale subjects as well as swans, storks, and turtle doves.

Chocolate

*T*T IS with the great Spanish explorers and conquistadores that the darkest chapter of confectionery begins. The cocoa tree, a demanding but generous everblooming tree growing in
Central America, was known to several indigenous tribes who used its
seeds in drinks, as money, and for sacrifices. In Aztec culture it was the
benevolent god Quetzalcoatl who had bestowed this precious gift on mankind,
and it was at the court of Montezuma II in 1519 that Hernando Cortez first saw
and drank the strange and bitter brew, made from the fermented, roasted, and
ground cocoa beans. He was less than thrilled by its taste, but wrote home about
this luxury food, which was served in golden goblets and apparently conferred
strength and sexual powers on its consumers. Since the seeds of the tree also served
as currency, Cortez established some cocoa plantations of his own in order to grow
money for the Spanish Crown. Upon Cortez's return home in 1528, his sovereign
king Charles V finally was able to sample some authentically prepared chocolate;
he thought the beverage could do with some sugar. So did the rest of Spain, and
before long, the whole of Europe. Or so the story goes.

The fact is that not only chocolate, but tea and coffee too, attained real popularity only once they were sweetened. Because the demand for sugar had been
steadily rising ever since its introduction to Europe from the Middle East,
Christopher Columbus decided to take some sugarcane stalks along on his second
trip to the West Indies in 1493, whereupon he gave the plants a try on different
soil. Botanically speaking the move was a triumph. In human terms, however, it
turned into a devastating tragedy. As sugar production is a labor-intensive process,

SANTA CLAUSES AND ANGELS
Approx. 4–9½" tall. Vanini, Lugano, Switzerland

*Just as there are good witches and bad witches,
so there is a kind Saint Nicholas and a fearsome
one, found in Nordic lore. Our beloved Saint
Nicholas—who was also the bishop of Myra
and the patron saint of sailors, unmarried girls,
bakers, apothecaries, pawnbrokers, and perfumers—would have been surprised to see his
own effigy in so many corny variations. These
jolly Santa Clauses, made in several steps involv-
ing four shades of chocolate, are all different versions of the above-mentioned benevolent saint.*

the successful experiment led to slavery and exploitation of such massive proportions that it is hard to understand how the pleasure of a few could be bought at the price of the sweat and the blood of so many. This pockmark on our collective conscience may well be why so much guilt is experienced when sugar is consumed.

With thus increased sugar supplies from the middle of the sixteenth century on, Europeans simply went crazy for the new beverage. The hot cocoa concoction, whisked until frothy (its Mexican name *Xocolatl* is supposedly of onomatopoetic origin, the "choco, choco, choco" imitating the sound of boiling chocolate being whipped with a wooden beater in an earthenware vessel or gourd), became the favorite pick-me-up of kings and queens, and probably of many a Don Giovanni who must have considered this elixir an important stepping stone in his act of seduction. Exceeding fashion chocolate became a cult and was drunk everywhere and all the time—in bed, at the table, in church, and places in between. Linnaeus gave it the noble name *Theobroma cocoa* (food of the gods), and its attraction did not wear off by any means when, several hundred years later, a method was found to convert it from a beverage into a solid edible bar. Many people today love chocolate with a passion that borders on religious fervor. Men "who don't like sweets" often confess that they do crave chocolate, as if addiction was a masculine trait which made a basic weakness acceptable. The addictive quality of chocolate has been compared to the chemistry of love and has been scrutinized by scientists. But the minimal amounts of caffeine, theobromine, and phenylethylamine it contains have been found negligible and appear in more concentrated form in other foods that have less of a grip on mankind. The answer for its unsurpassed popularity may simply be its taste. Solid chocolate is at its most delectable when mixed with cocoa butter and sugar, which means that it can satisfy three cravings at once: sugar, fat, and, what is its unique characteristic, an underlying bitter taste.

To get a solid chocolate that feels and tastes good is a complicated process, and it is not just a fluke that it had been so long in happening. Sooner or later every Latin country tried manufacturing chocolate, as did the English, the Belgians, and most successfully the Dutch, in the person of the chemist Conrad Van Houten, who in 1828 patented a screw press which could extract a large part of the 53 percent of the cocoa butter present in the chocolate beans. This made a less unctuous chocolate beverage possible, and it resulted in a lot of cocoa butter on the side. The stroke of genius came with the inspiration to incorporate extra cocoa butter into the somewhat rough chocolate paste made from the roasted, hulled, and crushed beans, a technique pioneered by the English firm Fry and Sons in Bristol in 1847. But ultimately the credit for processing chocolate is due to the Swiss Rodolphe Lindt, who devised a way and perfected the machinery able to work the extra cocoa butter into the chocolate during a long amalgamation process called conching, after which time all the unwanted volatile acids have evaporated and the warmed aromatic paste has become smooth as silk and can be cast into tablets that harden when cooled. Lindt's countrymen Cailler, Kohler, Peter, Nestlé, Suchard, and Sprüngli were all equally devoted to the principle that the quality of a good eating chocolate depended largely on its satiny texture and so built up their enterprises accordingly. Their success did not lie in some deeply guarded secret, but in the machinery required to roast, grind, mix, and refine the exotic raw materials. That chocolate is a high-tech product made possible by the age of industrialization is best illustrated by an advertisement of the reputed firm Caffarel in Turin, which in 1826 announced the acquisition of a new hydraulic machine for processing chocolate—not the quality of the chocolate itself.

HEART WITH KEYS
Heart: 5 x 5 x 3"; Longest key: 5". Zurich

A suggestive heart, made of hollow curved halves, was designed by a Swiss confectioner in reference to an early German poem in which eternal love is declared. A heart and keys are obviously meant as a gift to a sweetheart.

WRENCH, SCISSOR, PLIERS, AND FILE
Maximum length: 8" long. Zurich

The surreal set of life-size chocolate tools acquired its rusty look through a dusting of cocoa powder. A unique artifact, handmade by the same chocolatier who created the heart, it echoes its place of origin—a puritanical town with a pronounced work ethic.

CHOCOLATE TRAIN
Engine: 3½ x 1". Lindt & Sprüngli, Switzerland

Chocolate, railways, and tourism—the Swiss ingeniously combined all three with these milk chocolates that are boxed as sets, manufactured by one of the world's most respected firms.

SOUVENIR BLOCKS
1¾ x 1¾". Zurich

These milk and dark chocolate tablets are filled with chocolate cream centers and depict Zurich's landmarks in relief

SHEEP
Each sheep: 2" long. United States

One black sheep in a pen with nine white ones is an amusing gift item offered by an American catalogue house.

Today's chocolate factories are, of course, the height of sophistication, with automated processes, computerized recipes, electronic controls, and a special machine for every transaction. Even the molding of hollow Easter bunnies and Santa Clauses is fully mechanized. Warmed chocolate is poured into two-piece molds that are then placed into a machine which causes the chocolate to be distributed evenly over the inside of the two halves. After passing through a cooling tunnel the chocolate objects are removed by hand and then wrapped by another machine.

It was with the discovery of cocoa butter that chocolate joined the ranks of moldable materials. Cocoa butter is a miracle ingredient of sorts, a solid vegetable fat with the accommodating feature of turning liquid at precisely 92 degrees, which is just a few degrees below human body temperature; it thus melts away most voluptuously on our tongue. Astonishingly enough chocolate does not go rancid; kept under the right conditions a chocolate bar can stay good for a long time, years even, without refrigeration. With the idea to enrich chocolate with cocoa butter, the door was opened for a number of other additives, especially milk, thus solidifying Switzerland's chocolate fame and conferring upon chocolate an aura of wholesome goodness. In Italy, cocoa butter is sometimes blended with hazelnut paste to become gianduja, a specialty of Piedmont. But chocolate's most constant companion is another gift from the Aztec world, also brought by Cortez along with silver, gold, and jewels—vanilla. The black, fragrant, leathery stick sold in specialty shops is the seedpod of an orchid, and like chocolate is a tropical crop requiring great care. The vanilla blossom, for instance, has to be hand pollinated on the one short day on which the orchid blooms, while the football-shaped seedpod of the cocoa tree must be carefully removed by hand when ripe without damage to the remaining fruit and blossoms. Curiously enough, neither chocolate nor vanilla, which we love for their rich perfume, have any odor when attached to the plant; fermentation brings about their seductive fragrance. For this phenomenon we are indebted to the early Mesoamerican natives for their keen interest and noses; without them we might never have come to enjoy these exquisite substances.

In an industry with serious goals and objectives, chocolate producers have worked at expanding their market and have achieved this by extending the retail sweet, season from Christmas to Easter. Of all figurative sweets, Easter rabbits and Easter eggs are probably the most widespread and are produced by the tens of thousands. Valentine's Day is a celebratory day dreamt up by retailers to keep things rolling between winter and spring, allowing the vendors to cash in on chocolate's age-old aphrodisiac connotations.

As a sweet complement or token of love, chocolate has taken on the role gingerbread once had. Long before Hershey's kisses and Perugina's baci, the old Johann Wolfgang Goethe, still a suitor at the age of eighty, sent a box of chocolates to his nineteen-year-old love Ulrike with a little poem, a gift he dispatched from the spa town of Karlsbad in Austria. As it happened, the budding chocolate industry coincided with an increase in tourism in Central Europe, and chocolate sales have remained a spin-off of the tourist trade. Not everybody traveling through Switzerland is ready and willing to buy a cuckoo clock, but most foreigners find it hard to resist stocking up on chocolate before going home. In Switzerland, chocolate is also a classic pocket food of mountaineers and hikers, for as Alexander von Humboldt correctly assessed, chocolate is a phenomenon of concentrated nourishment. It was for this reason that the Hershey company produced high-energy chocolate bars for the American army during World War II.

One would think that such credentials should suffice to recommend this desirable sweet in its basic form, but chocophiles, afficionados, and devotees forever long for further refinements. The chocolatier is the person who lavishly caters to his sybaritic clientele with handmade cream truffles, bonbons laced with liqueurs, and other delicate hand-dipped morsels. Experience and know-how are prerequisites of his profession, for chocolate is a temperamental prima donna who has to be handled with great respect. Chocolate making is largely a series of warming and cooling processes, which must be carried out extremely carefully, as chocolate scorches easily, which gives it an objectionable flavor. Its texture is given to strange antics when handled improperly, and it can become lumpy, grainy, or waxy. When melting chocolate, a splash of water can cause the chocolate to seize, and when casting it into molds, it has to be tempered, which is to say it has to be heated, stirred, and cooled in a disciplined way, so that it takes on an appetizing glossy sheen. The chocolatier often works with special types of chocolate of varying fat content, such as *couverture* and *ganache,* for covering or filling petit fours or candies

As chocolate is a relatively recent material, its iconography is unburdened by tradition and is full of unconventional shapes, which are often cast as simple pieces. Once in a while one comes across more complex works assembled from smaller castings, such as Palladian villas, which served as fantastic table decorations or as window displays. For many a young chocolatier, this exacting blend of culinary and architectural skills is often the final step on the ladder of his apprenticeship.

EASTER RABBITS
Overall range: 3½–16″. From various countries

A group of Easter rabbits in every type of chocolate and range of sizes demonstrates the enduring popularity of this animal, which is the most widespread of all figurative sweets. As a potent symbol of procreation, the hare has managed to stay around forever. He was originally an attribute of Eastre, the Teutonic goddess of dawn who inspired the holiday.

EASTER RABBIT'S HELPER
5½", Germany

Companion piece to the rabbit at right.

EASTER RABBIT
7" tall, Germany

More a hare than a rabbit, this white chocolate Easter confection made from an antique mold appears in a somewhat humanized version. Various degrees of anthropomorphic features, such as garments, add the fairyland reality that children adore.

INSECT
7" long. Switzerland

Dozens of these insects known as Maikäfer *pop up in Swiss bakeries during the month of May. They come in miniature as well as in sizes up to 20 inches long. Body and wings, cast as separate pieces in milk and dark chocolate, are convincingly joined together; cardboard legs complete them. The inspiration was probably provided by the Katzenjammer Kids who had good fun with bugs, chocolate or otherwise.*

(OPPOSITE) LARGE FISH AND MINIATURE CREATURES
Miniatures approx. 1" long; fish: 10" long. Paris

Hollow chocolate fish filled with miniature sea creatures, also in chocolate, appear on April Fools' Day, which in France is known as poisson d'avril. *As a sign of the zodiac, as a primitive symbol of Christianity, and as a sacred animal in many cultures, the fish has been used in decorations of every conceivable nature.*

LOVE LETTERS
6″ high, New York

PINK LIPS
3½″ wide, New York

All letters of the alphabet are available, but these four are the best-sellers. They were handcrafted in New York from Belgian chocolate and for a while were sold in handsome boxes, the same way that individualized messages piped onto chocolate blackboards were.

Lush, pink chocolate lips speak for America's innovative spirit. The fascination with white chocolate, which is basically just cocoa butter with sugar and some milk solids, has given American chocolatiers the idea to add new colors to chocolate's formerly limited palette.

NAKED LADY
7 x 4". New York

Old subject matter, new treatment. Nudity had its ups and downs in the evolution of sweets. Pre-Christian gingerbread was quite explicit. After that, Adam and Eve and mythological figures served as models. Later, dress codes claimed the public's interest, so carvers of lebkuchen molds copied fashions of the time. Today, nakedness is again in vogue. This pin-up girl, made of dark chocolate, was bought in Times Square in New York and clearly addresses herself to a male public.

Candy

ORE than any other operation in the kitchen, working with sugar is a precise science requiring the experience and skill of a professional. Candy making is controlled chemistry; directions have to be carried out to the letter. While it is difficult to botch up gingerbread dough or to fail with marzipan, attempting to make real fondant can easily result in a mess, not only hard to clean up but nearly impossible to eat or even reuse. The same is true when producing other kinds of confections, like clear candy, for instance—a single crystal forming too soon in the wrong place leads inevitably to disappointment, for the opposite of what one aimed for has happened and the sugar has become dull and cloudy.

Depending on its moisture content the consistency of sugar can vary from rock hard to creamy. It can look transparent like glass, shiny like silk, opaque like stone. To the touch, it is brittle and gritty, smooth and velvety, or moist and chewy. These variations are achieved by controlling the way in which boiled sugar syrup cools and solidifies. Other than the ineptitude of the cook, working with sugar has only one natural enemy: humidity, which renders certain procedures impossible and turns completed objects into sorry sights of gooey disintegration. This was already remarked upon in the sixteenth century when sugar was becoming more widely available due to augmented imports from Caribbean plantations. A hundred years later, in the age of Descartes, sugar was available in sufficient quantities to warrant the codification of the stages at which sugar boils. Since then, the candy thermometer has become the confectioner's essential tool for measuring the tem-

MISCELLANEOUS CANDIES
White silk cushion: 3/8 x 1/4", 1" diameter.
From various countries

Candies culled from many different countries are made in the shape of tiny objects such as berries, silk cushions, flowers, and ice. Most of them have fruit flavors, but some contain herbal ingredients such as licorice or mint, harking back to the Middle Ages when sugar was used for medicinal purposes.

perature of the boiling liquid, thus indicating the ratio of sugar to water, expressed on a scale graduating from 158° to 392° Fahrenheit. An experienced practitioner will know from the look of the bubbling syrup what stage it is in; further tests can be done with a glass of cold water into which a bit of boiling sugar is dribbled and then studied for its consistency. The numerous stages thus identified are testimony to sugar's adaptable chemistry: small gloss or small thread, large gloss or small thread, small pearl, large pearl, small soufflé, large soufflé, small ball, large ball, light crack, crack, hard crack, and caramel.

Three groups of candy are made by boiling a sugar and water solution to a certain degree and cooling it in different ways. There is the crystalline type, of which rock candy and fondant are typical examples. The noncrystalline sort comprises hard candy, so-called barley sugar, taffy, and chewy caramel, among others. A third type is obtained by adding a binding agent to the sugar syrup, such as gelatin, starch, pectin, or a plant gum, especially gum arabic, which is a product gained from the bark of certain acacia trees. These substances help the sugar solution to jell, with or without adding a taste of their own. Jelly beans, Turkish delight, and licorice are all examples.

Other candies can be made by combining any of the above with each other, such as by encasing a soft center in a coating of hard sugar, or by adding seeds, nuts, chocolate, marzipan, and candied fruit, some of which are themselves candies in their own right. Mixing beaten egg white and honey with warm sugar forms the base for nougat and torrone, to which almonds and hazelnuts are commonly added. Caramelizing ground nuts yields praline, named in honor of the Duc du Plessis-Praslin, a commander of the French army under Louis XIII. Caramelized almond chips poured or rolled into a large sheet while warm are called nougatine. In the past this was the patissier's most indispensable mate-

rial for making baskets, urns, cornucopias, and more complicated constructions. Regrettably this attractive technique is on the brink of extinction as it requires a great deal of patience, time, and a high degree of skill.

The oldest sorts of candy were sugar-coated seeds or nuts called *dragées* or *confits*. These are none other than the ancestors of the *confetti* (meaning Jordan almonds—fine almonds originating from Malaga), sent around in Italy and France to announce a wedding or the birth of a child. From the Datini papers, the miraculously preserved fourteenth-century records made by the rich merchant from Prato, we know that in Florence at that time it was customary for a godfather to bring eight pounds of white comfits, one pound of red comfits, two heavy cakes, and an assortment of candles and torches to the christening of a godchild. The most popular comfits were sugared anise and coriander seeds, pine nuts, ginger, and fenugreek, some of which occasionally can still be found today. Usually these were served at the end of a sumptuous meal.

Like all rare foods, such sugar preparations were initially proclaimed to function as medicine and act as aphrodisiacs. They were dispensed by apothecaries in the form of so-called electuaries. These electuaries were supposed to alleviate an endless list of ailments and for hundreds of years were believed to fortify the stomach, quiet the heat of the belly, cool the liver, warm the kidneys, stimulate the spleen, reduce the humidity of the head and the vapors of the brain, purge phlegm, assuage dryness of the tongue, mouth, throat, and windpipe, improve breath, and legions more. And while we may smile at such naiveté, let us not overlook the fact that the cough drops and throat lozenges we suck are their legitimate heirs, or that the licorice pastilles many French and Italians hanker after are actually aids in digestion.

The essential oils of many herbs and plants known for their tonic, stimulant, diuretic, or expectorant effects have

been affixed to sugar. Peppermint, sarsaparilla, wintergreen, hyssop, anise, angelica, horehound (mentioned already by Hypocrates), eucalyptus, cinnamon, marshmallow, barberries, Icelandic moss, to name just a small number of many, are not only esteemed for their refreshing or soothing properties but as distinct enrichments of our gamut of tastes. Without sugar we could hardly enjoy the bizarre taste of angelica, the matchless aroma of cinnamon, or the pungent flavor of eucalyptus. Thus, to the true gourmet, the marvelous characteristic of sugar is by no means just its sweetness, but its ability to carry and amplify the taste of the ingredients it is mixed with. Sugar acts as a fixative and preserver of otherwise elusive flavors, as, incidentally, do certain liqueurs. And indeed, confectionary, preserving, and distillation went hand in hand and were branches of the same profession for centuries.

To candy also means to preserve fruit by boiling it with sugar; in doing so it also tenderizes woody or inedible parts of fruit, such as orange peel or melon rind. It is here that cane sugar won out over honey after 1600, as honey does not lend itself to making preserves and is less easy to store. The purer the sugar the better the marmalades and jellies, which is hardly a consideration for the modern cook, but which was a prime concern of every housekeeper before 1900, as sugar was manufactured in different grades. The most refined was of course also the most expensive; cookbooks from the period gave the necessary directions for clarifying lesser varieties.

In the modern world, jellies, candied fruit, and fruit pastes have lost some of their impact, and dinner guests would be pretty stunned today if they were served nothing but a little pot of jam with a spoon for dessert, even if it were of violets or roses. Yet in the not-so-distant past, palates were less jaded and many flavors were strictly seasonal and much purer. To taste preserved raspberries in the middle of winter was sensational. Today, we have become oblivious to such unique tastes because fast transportation and freezers have cheated nature (and us) of the seasonal appearance of various foods.

Many candies have the desirable virtue of staying in the mouth a little longer than other foods. Since one of mankind's favorite activities is chewing, there was yet room for another form of candy, whose jaw-exercising texture was later approved of by psychologists and manufacturers alike: chewing gum. Before Chicle gum was patented in 1871, various resins, bee waxes, tobacco, and latexes secreted by plants filled the need for incessant mastication in different corners of the world. The renowned and uncommonly perceptive writer M. F. K. Fisher once wrote that the bright taste of tar peeled from the freshly paved street in her hometown of Whittier, California, was "much better than anything put out by Wrigley or Beechnut," and was the forbidden fruit she and her sister secretly relished in their childhood. The gum we know today apparently owes its existence to a Mexican general by the name of Antonio López de Santa Anna, who habitually chewed the tasteless resin of the sapodilla tree, known by its Aztec name *Chictli*. Despite his famous attack on Fort Alamo, the general was later allowed to settle in Staten Island, New York, where he brought a good deal of his native *Chictli*. With the help of American ingenuity, commercial spirit, and Thomas Adams, the *Chictli* resin was gradually developed into the chewing gum we are only too familiar with today. Since it supposedly releases facial tension, gum is even included in field rations for American soldiers.

As candies are considered small pleasures and are eaten without the excuse of a special event or ceremony, they do not require elaborate artistic guises. On the level of everyday consumption we encounter a modest assortment of emblematic little eggs and babies, fruits and acorns, or the shape

CANDY PLATES
Approx. 1¾–4½", United States

Wonderful glasslike objects such as these miniature plates can be made by boiling sugar, water, glucose, and food coloring to 290 degrees and pouring the liquid into oiled molds to set.

SHIP
6¾" high, Charles Regennas, Lititz, Pennsylvania

Blue is the most difficult color to achieve in this type of candy because the caramel color of the boiling sugar is likely to mar it. Mr. Regennas, a retired mailman who has made clear candy for decades from his collection of 19th-century inherited German pewter molds, knows how to overcome such problems.

CAMEL
5". Charles Regennas, Lititz, Pennsylvania

The camel rests on a dune of unrefined sugar which does not lend itself to candy making; only the purest white granulated sugar will give the desired results. This type of candy is sometimes referred to as barley sugar or sucre d'orge, which is a misnomer. Barley has nothing to do with it.

RABBITS
5". Charles Regennas, Lititz, Pennsylvania

SUGAR TOYS
2–3½″ high. Charles Regennas, Lititz, Pennsylvania

Mr. Regennas makes these clear sugar toys in a workshop near his home. A few years back he still sold his smallest handmade items and lollipops to schoolchildren for a nickel apiece. In earlier, more austere days, toys like these were often the only Christmas gifts children got. They were hung on the tree and remained there until Twelfth Night (or Epiphany), when the goodies were taken down and distributed. Kittens in a slipper and boot, various dogs, a fox who stole a goose, an eagle, a policeman, an owl in a tree, a soldier on horseback, a frog on a bicycle are all derived from the world of German children's songs and stories.

of the flower or berry whose natural flavors provided the candy's taste. At the pinnacle of the confectioner's profession, however, are the sparkling displays of pulled, poured, spun, or blown sugar. These pieces are the virtuoso acts performed only by a handful of artisans who draw on their own imaginations to create the large, three-dimensional show pieces which are in spirit, though probably not in looks, the contemporary versions of the former *trionfi di tavola,* or sculpted sugar objects. They serve as the focus of prestigious occasions, such as Julia Child's 80th birthday, for instance, when master confiseur André Renard presented her with a nearly life-sized cooking stove, with pots and pans and tiled surroundings, all made of sugar, much of it blown.

Blowing sugar is a technique that obeys laws similar to glass blowing. First, sugar is heated to a high degree and then poured onto a marble slab, where it is repeatedly pulled and stretched. It is next formed into a ball and is blown under a hot lamp, with the help of a pipe and a good pair of lungs, to the size of a vase or jug. It is a method often used to form amusing puppets, which populate stage sets made entirely out of sugar, eliciting wonder and mirth, as did their precursors in the heyday of sugar sculpture during the Renaissance.

Of a more practical and unexpected nature are certain sugar objects produced by specialists for dramatic use. When cowboy actors "crash" through windowpanes, or when a happy tenor exuberantly smashes his wineglass on stage, safety dictates that the fragile item in question be made not of glass but of sugar, which is usually poured or blown. On a theatrical occasion of a different kind, a substitute for leather was found in toothsome licorice for the infamous scene in the *Gold Rush,* where Charlie Chaplin and his cabin mate eat a boiled shoe. Since the scene had to be reshot forty times, no doubt the licorice shoe took its toll on the digestive system of its diners.

COLLECTION OF BIRDS' EGG CANDIES
3/4–1 1/4". Various countries

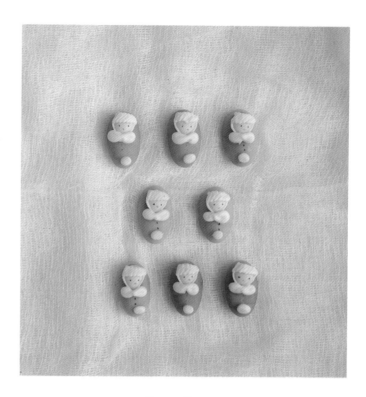

SUGAR BABIES
1 1/4". Switzerland

The egg is a universally accepted cosmic symbol, expressing the mystery of life, rebirth, and immortality. Candy eggs come in a multitude of materials, sizes, and colors. Some of these specimens are American candies called malted eggs. The others come from Germany, Mexico, and France, and are filled with nougat and chocolate.

Children's trinkets or descendants of ancient rituals? Swaddled babies were made of gingerbread and given out at 17th-century weddings as undisguised allusions to future tidings.

AMERICAN FLAG CANDY BOX
Box: 5 x 7½". United States

MEDALLION OF INDIAN HEAD
1½ x 2¼". Vermont

Star-shaped fondant candies were arranged in a box to resemble the American flag for the bicentennial of the United States in 1976. A hundred years earlier, Philadelphia had produced walnut Liberty Bell candies as a similarly celebratory confection.

Maple sugar candy has a distinct flavor and place of origin, as suggested by the Indian head and maple leaves. Maple candy is made by extracting the sap from the maple tree and boiling off the excess water—the same way sugar is made from sugar cane or beets.

(OPPOSITE) LICORICE COLLECTION
Pipe: 4"; spider: 1¼"; smallest baby: ¾". Italy, France, and
United States

The ominous language of licorice is full of allusions to such masculine accoutrements as pipes, rockets, tanks, and weapons. Black spiders and insects are common at Halloween, while the pieces of coal on the upper left belong to the Befana, a type of Italian female Santa Claus or witch who appears on January 6 to reward good children with gifts and punish bad ones with "coals." Shoelaces, black sugar babies, and bingo chips add to the mystery of these hieroglyphs.

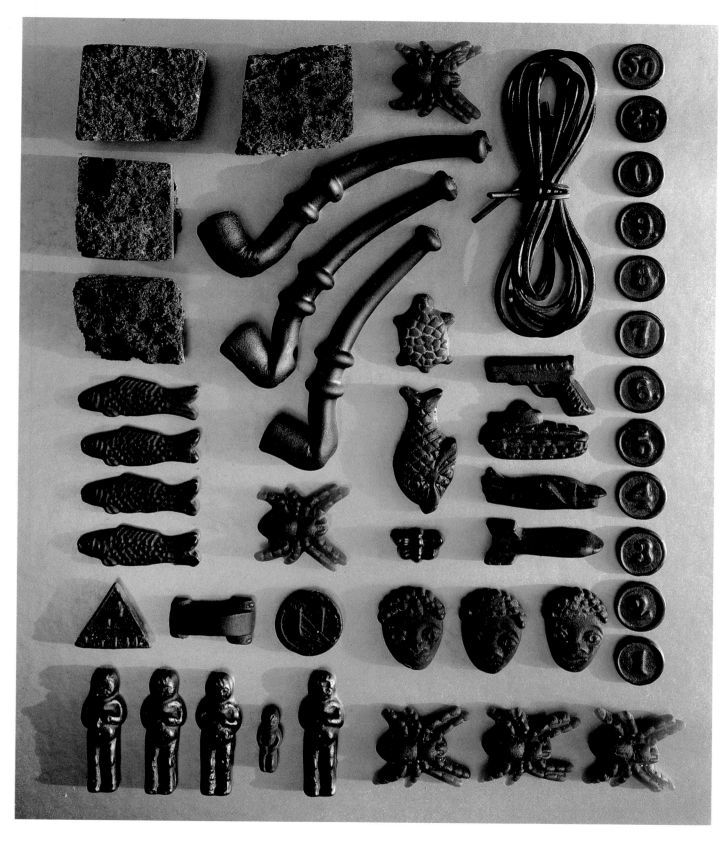

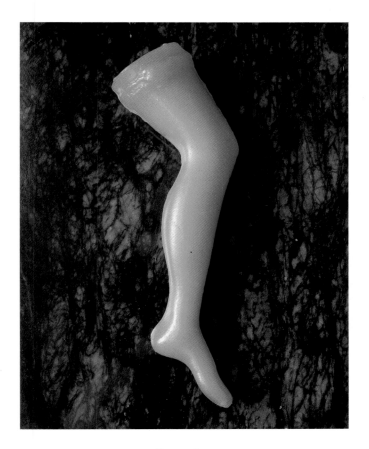

CANDY LEG
5″. From an English seaside resort

LAUREL AND HARDY LOLLIPOPS
8″ (without stick). France

(OPPOSITE) CHEWING GUM
Cigar: 4¼″: cigarillo: 4½″. United States

Bubble gum cigars, chewing gum and chocolate cigarettes, as well as
candy cigarillos are macho fare for little boys.

SAUSAGES, LOOPS, AND DECORATIVE SHAPES
Loop: 2½". Switzerland

Sausages, loops, and ornamental shapes made of quince paste are traditional Christmas fare in Switzerland and other countries bound to old-fashioned practices. Quince paste is among the oldest of all confections. In 15th-century Portugal it went under the name of marmalade. The earliest recipes list rosewater and musk among the ingredients, which would indicate that, like marzipan, it was a sweetmeat of Eastern origin.

HAZELNUTS, ALMONDS, AND OLIVES
1–1¼". Paris

Deceptively real-looking almonds, hazelnuts, and olives are actually crunchy bonbons with praline fillings.

(OPPOSITE) FRUITS, VEGETABLES, AND BABIES
Approx. ½–1½". Portugal

Portuguese candies in the shape of little fruits, flowers, and babies come into play at Eastertime and are the typical symbols meant to propitiate the forces of nature and encourage fertility.

RASPBERRIES
½″ high. Sweden

Raspberry jellies coated in sugar pearls.

FONDANT FLOWERS
United States

VIOLETS
⁷/₈″ high. France

An old-fashioned flower with the same old-fashioned flavor.

APPLE AND APPLE BLOSSOM ON A PLATE
Apple: 4¼" diameter. Marguerite Lapierre, Paris

This apple still life is designed as part of a wedding table decoration and was made in blown sugar, a technique that this great Parisian specialist learned from glass blowers in Venice.

SUGAR PLATE WITH BLOSSOM
6¾" diameter. Marguerite Lapierre, Paris

For her sugar decorations Mme. Lapierre invented a secret formula that allowed her to produce these sugar artifacts which neither become sticky nor disintegrate as other sugar objects normally do when exposed to humid conditions.

(OPPOSITE) SUGAR PLATE WITH CHERRIES
7" diameter. Marguerite Lapierre, Paris

Another creation by Mme. Lapierre in the vein of medieval puzzle food. Both plate and cherries are edible—if necessary.

DIAMONDS, HEARTS, CLUBS, AND SPADES
1". Czechoslovakia

Sugar lumps in the shape of diamonds, hearts, clubs, and spades are sold under the name of "Bridge Sugar."

(OPPOSITE) SATIN BOW
10" long, 6" wide. André Renard, France

This satin bow is as delicious to eat as it is luscious to look at. It was made in pulled sugar (sucre tiré) by a maître patissier for whom sugar seems to have no limitations.

Mexico and Japan

MEXICO and Japan, with their extraordinarily diverse cultures and religions, are each distinguished by their unusual claim on sugar. Both countries produce sweets that are unmistakably theirs, and whose function in their society is more than culinary satisfaction. For the Mexicans, as for the Japanese, sweets serve as enforcements of traditional values and religious rituals, and are, or can be, forms of national self-identification. In this way, confections serve to preserve an aspect of cultural heritage—something not even modernization or Westernization can truly erode.

The production of sweets with symbolic meaning is of course more dense in some parts of the world than in others. Secluded regions with a strong agricultural background and pronounced folklore are more likely to produce breads and confections embodying the ritual roles of food than areas shaped by outside influences and heavy industrialization.

Switzerland is one such region that brims with sweets of every sort, a fact due to that country's traditionalist attitude and to a proliferation of professional confectioners. Switzerland's sugar bakers flourished at home or emigrated abroad, especially the ones born in the poor mountain areas of Graubünden, seeking their luck in the world at large. During the 1700s and 1800s, they spread all over Europe and through natural talent and diligence established a virtual network of pastry shops and coffeehouses; with their fortunes in hand, many of them returned home.

Sicily is another region whose inhabitants are similarly attached to native soil and local customs. Like Switzerland, it too had a role as a purveyor of sweets to

FLOWER BOUQUET IN BLUE VASE
6 x 8 x 1". Toraya, Tokyo

The vase filled with two peonies, chrysanthe-mums, and cherry blossoms is a special-order item from the famous shop Toraya in Tokyo. This sugar-and-rice-flour confection, made in a wooden mold, serves as a congratulatory gift for a joyous event. Since it dries to a hard candy, it can be kept for a long time.

the world at large, in particular as the springboard for the Arabian concept of sweetmeats, and in more recent times as the cradle of ice cream.

To the ethnologist or anthropologist, however, Mexico is the country that takes the cake, so to speak, for its wealth of sugar artifacts radiate with religious, magical, and superstitious associations, and denote a more palpable layering of cultures than is visible elsewhere. In the Old World, many cultures died out or were modified by changes wrought by war or economic upheaval, just as they were in Central and South America. But more time has elapsed since the Christian faith imposed its imprint on Northern Europe, for example, whose conversion was effected between the sixth and eighth centuries, whereas Mexico was tackled by missionary fervor as recently as four hundred and fifty years ago, and thus shows clearer vestiges of a previous civilization.

The Aztec culture the conquistadores found was actually a highly sophisticated one, and the Spaniards were dazzled by many discoveries, such as Emperor Montezuma II's banquets, noteworthy not only for the precious vessels and elaborate utensils, but for their culinary riches as well. Though unfamiliar with cane sugar, the Mesoamerican natives clearly had a sweet tooth, which gave rise to more than three hundred different dishes prepared with wild honeys, fruit and corn syrups, and an extract from the Maguey plant called *aguamiel* (honey water), which when fermented yields the famous *pulque*. With the advent of Christianity, milk and cane sugar were added to this list of ingredients, much promoted by the monasteries, which became the leading producers of specialty sweets. Here as elsewhere the Church took over more than the local food and recipes; it also absorbed the customs and holidays of the subjugated pagans and integrated them into its own calendar of saints.

One such day in Mexico's life is the Dia de los Muertes, which is a fusion between the Catholic All Souls and All Saints Day and the festivities of Mictlantecuhtli, the God of Death, when the Aztecs commemorated the dead. Even in modern Mexico it is a day of capital importance. Preparations are made long before the first and second of November, when the souls of the dead come to pay their annual visit and seek comfort among the living. The whole nation is humming like a beehive in anticipation of the fiesta to come. The houses are scrubbed, holy water is fetched, ample supplies of flowers, candles, ribbons, paper cut outs, and sugar sculptures are bought. Food is prepared, which is offered as nourishment for the dead and as a way of affirming remembrance of loved ones. To display the *Ofrendas per los Muertes* (the offerings to the dead), a table is placed outside the front door, bedecked with candles and the traditional sweet breads, the *pan de los muertes,* which are decorated with motifs based on the human skeleton. Added to these are the mysterious *calaveras,* or sugar skulls, each individualized with a paper headband inscribed with someone's name. Platters of tamales and *pollo en mole* are set out along with other favorite dishes as offerings for the deceased. Set at the foot of the table is a little straw mat decorated with a border of flower petals. On it are exhibited the deceased's tools of his trade, as are his preferences or weaknesses in the form of a jug of *pulque,* a bottle of Tequila, or a pack of cigarettes.

During the night of November 1 a vigil is kept in the town cemetery, where the revelers assemble around the modest graves adorned for the occasion with candles and flowers. They have not come to wail or cry; they have gathered to keep the invisible spirits company and to assure them that they have not been forgotten. The vigil is solemn though relaxed. There is praying and chattering, children playing, an exchange of gossip and food. To a North American the atmosphere comes across as a mix between a Fourth of July picnic and the funeral of a distant relative.

FRUIT
2½″ diameter. Puebla

Set on a small silver plate, this pomegranate, mandarin, and other fruits are made out of pumpkin seed paste, Mexico's equivalent of marzipan, which is somewhat coarser in texture but equally malleable and nutritious. Fruit and seeds are in-trinsic harvest motifs worldwide. They induce gods and spirits to bestow fertility on future crops.

MINIATURE SUGAR PLATES, FRUIT BASKETS, AND FRUIT
2–3″ diameter. Puebla

Miniature sugar plates of sugar paste and fondant candy in the shape of tortillas, fried eggs, coffee cups, fruit baskets, sugar cane, and tropical fruit are edible dollhouse paraphernalia put out for the souls of the dead children on the Day of the Dead.

GUNS AND WAFERS
Gunz: ¾", Mexico City

Machine-made candies in the form of handguns come in the same rainbow colors as the wafers joined together with caramel.

COLORED FONDANT CANDIES WITH ICING
1½–2", Mexico City

Mexican motifs such as sombreros and guitars join the widespread symbols of baskets, lambs, and crosses, all of which make their appearance for the Day of the Dead. The rectangular-shaped candy is a metate, the stone on which the flour for tortillas is ground.

Festivities for deceased children precede those for adults, held on the afternoon of October 31, when the families gather in the courtyards of their houses, and reverently sip chocolate and place their *ofrendas* on the small altarlike table. There, *muertitos chicos,* or souls of the dead children, find not only food but also little toys on their tables. The idea of sweetening their short stay on earth is literal, for most of the toys are made of sugar. During the past weeks, thousands and thousands of these objects have been created and carried to market. At this time most of the markets have become so crowded that some stands have spilled out onto the street, where rows of tables are given over to the *alfeñiques,* the sugar toys made especially for the Dia de los Muertes. Onlookers and clients study all the merchandise very carefully, lovingly choosing the best and most beautiful among hundreds. They assemble their selections on tin trays, which may include a skull bearing the name of a friend, or an open coffin with a skeleton set within. When the transaction is concluded the faithful hurry home, their purchases wrapped in a little hay or newspaper or whatever else is at hand. Their faces radiate excitement, while the little children soothe their impatience sucking broken pieces of sweets. And breakage there is, for all the *alfeñiques*—made from a mixture of egg white, flour, and sugar—are as fragile as glass. In the end, all of them get eaten, for when the second day of November is over the dead souls will have absorbed the essence of the food, drink, and toys, and have generously left them behind for the enjoyment of the living.

What is most notable about the Dia de los Muertes is not the communion between the living and the dead per se, which after all has equivalents elsewhere, but the ubiquitous presence of the human skeleton as a decorative feature— without the kind of abstraction that has taken place in other cultures. Hard cookies jokingly referred to as "dead man's bones" (*croquants des morts*), and so on, exist in various other countries, but have not retained the shape of the human tibia or vertebrae. And funeral biscuits, where they still exist, at most carry stylized insignias like plumes, hearts, or roses that have none of the horrors or direct intimations of death. It is the Mexicans' cozy familiarity with the human anatomy that makes the outsider wonder if this vernacular is not per chance the residue of a more barbaric past, when human sacrifice was a regular ritual, c. 1500 A.D., as witnessed by the conquistadores. At that time, the showing of still pulsating hearts was followed by cannibal meals, where those of high social standing were presented with the choice cuts, while the lower classes made stews of the remaining body parts.

One suspects that not to observe the return of the dead souls would be tantamount to bringing bad luck on one's head. This belief even occurs in North America in the "Trick or Treat" tradition of Halloween, whereby children disguised as ghosts and witches knock on doors as ambassadors from another world and ask for treats. If not placated by candy these young demons will take revenge and play nasty tricks on the offending host. A similar gesture of appeasement is the milk and cookies put out on the fireplace or windowsill for Santa Claus, who, as one recalls, has his dark origins too, and who in any case is a good person to have on one's side and should be treated kindly. Thus, what was once the anxious concern of adults has not been totally eliminated but has been relegated to the realm of childhood. For childhood, in many ways a recapitulation of our early evolution, serves as the archive for beliefs or emotions no longer found useful, but which we do not want to give up completely.

If Mexico's approach to sweets has a distinctly irreverent side, Japan is impressive for the earnestness it brings to its confections. Japanese food is altogether famous for its visual appeal; its sweets are almost spiritual, extremely beauti-

ANGEL, BABY, AND ANIMALS
Angel: 3½". Coatepec de Harinas

In this group of pumpkin seed paste figures assembled in a mangerlike arrangement, the infant Jesus is guarded by an angel. The surrounding group is somewhat less orthodox: a fish, dog, lamb, and rabbit. Like all the other Mexican sweets illustrated in this chapter, they pertain to the festivities of November 1 and 2.

RAM, STAGS, AND A PIG
Approx. 3–7" high. Toluca

These toy animals, or alfeñiques, made of sugar paste with inedible silver sprinkles, are a perfect example of the mingling of different cultures. Artifacts of horned animals are frequently found in primitive cultures. Here they have been aligned with the reindeer of Northern Christmas lore.

ful, and utterly foreign to a large part of the world. Pierre Loti (1850–1923), the French novelist who poured his passion for Japan into the two novels *Madame Chrystanthème* and *La Troisième Jeunesse de Madame Prune,* had to confess that the pink-colored sweetmeats flavored with pepper that he was offered at teatime tasted strange and unfamiliar and presented no temptation to the Western palate. Many people agree with this and have never acquired a taste for any of these Japanese sweets. But the physical appearance of wagashi and other foods is exquisite by anyone's standards and bespeaks the refined sense of aesthetics that suffuses Japanese culture. Aesthetic Japanese philosophy requires that all objects be beautiful, no matter whether large or small, expensive or cheap. This love for the delightful and inexpensive is clearly expressed in their enticing candy boxes, whether found in small market towns or in large department stores. Considerable if sometimes intrinsic meaning can be packed into a small package of sweets, as in the case of one confection bought in a tiny shop in Kyoto. There, the business had been handed down from father to son for seventeen generations, along with the recipe of two delicate types of candies flavored with some unusual fermented bean paste—the only two products sold in the store. A five hundred-year-old taste treat is a rare thing and should be considered money well spent.

The Japanese care deeply for nature, and their awareness of the changing seasons is a key element that pervades their whole culture, from Haiku poems to dress code, tableware, textile designs, and cuisine. Each season is expressed by a set of symbols, some of them readily comprehensible, such as blossoms, autumn leaves, and fruit, while others are less easy to interpret.

Distinctions are made between even such subtle changes as early spring to spring to early summer, each phase "described" by its own motifs. The careful coordination of sweets with these is practically second nature to the Japanese confectioner. Boxes with assorted higashi, that is to say dry, brittle candies made in molds from sugar paste, are assembled in slightly different colors or motifs that vary from one season to another. To the uninitiated the difference is hard to see, and if not familiar with Japanese symbolism one may not be able to determine to what time of year a box belongs. The usually monochromatic tiny candies come in tender pastel colors and enchant with their extremely fine reliefs of irises, persimmons, bundles of bamboo, and similar symbols borrowed from the rich arsenal of Japanese designs.

Wagashi, the collective noun for all sweets, comprise a broader range of confections than do higashi, and are usually somewhat larger and softer. It goes without saying that seasonal appropriateness is of the essence here too. Though sometimes referred to as tea cakes, they are not cakes as we know them, but cakes in the sense of patties or molded pieces. Wagashi developed alongside the tea ceremony, which means that the depth of their refined beauty has been contemplated for hundreds of years. These cautiously sweetened delicacies often look like opaque, glistening jewels, two to four inches in diameter at the most. They are made from pastes or doughs composed of such substances as boiled azuki beans, glutinous rice flours, red bean jams, agar agar, wheat or millet flour, and sugar, the latter preferably made in Japan. Their texture is as important as their taste— they can be soft, moist, crisp, gummy, or gelatinous, either throughout or in any combination. They are formed by hand and steamed, or pressed into wooden molds to become dry sweets, and they come in an infinite number of shades and variations in a palette of muted colors that one can instantly recognize as Japanese, just as Mexico's gay magentas and turquoises are likewise readily identified with their culture.

The prestigious firm Toraya, which has existed since 1600, has over three thousand wagashi recipes. One of its most popular is *monaka,* a moist azuki bean filling encased in white or pink wafers pressed into the shape of cherry blossoms or chrysanthemums. Another well-known type sold in bars is *yokan,* a shiny, rubbery bean paste product that vaguely resembles the French *marrons glacées* minus the sugar. Others, called *nerikiri,* are made to order in bigger and more prestigious shapes. Packed into fine cedar wood boxes, these traditional sweets are given for ceremonial purposes, such as weddings and funerals, and are made in the stylized form of cranes, lotus flowers, chrysanthemums, and turtles, or whatever symbol the occasion calls for. The Japanese love of detail and the artistic care dispensed on them is evident in each and every one of them, and their pristine freshness and exquisite elegance speak volumes. A beautiful box completes these artifacts with further symbolic significance and tells a story of its own.

Just like the intense awareness of nature, packaging too is a form of cultural heritage in Japan and goes beyond utilitarian considerations. In the West as in the East, sweets are considered luxuries and are usually offered as gifts. Japanese gift wrapping differs from ours, as it is not meant to hide but rather to enhance the content of the package, which to the Japanese is instantly recognizable from the outside. The consummate skill which goes into making a package in Japan is an expression of respect for the objects themselves and is meant to put one into a contemplative mood. The preciousness of wagashi or higashi is underlined by the frame of the attractive box. Strings and papers in tell-tale colors denote the spirit in which the present is given. Western commerce has worked out color combinations signifying specific events too: orange and black stand for Halloween, red and green for Christmas, yellow and purple for Easter. But these do not have the same impact as the meaning of color has in Japan, where it is, or originally was, experienced on a more monotone background, whereas our lives are already too colorful as it is.

To wrap it all up, confections are not disappearing from our lives, but they are changing. Evolution goes on, even in the dreamland of sweets. Mass-produced packaging is more often a substitute for old handcrafted objects, just as chocolate has come to replace the function gingerbread once had. A vague meaning of talismanic significance is occasionally still conveyed, and sometimes the commitment to quality and experience is expressed in keeping an old-fashioned label as its own best advertisement. Old habits die hard, and there is reason to hope that the best of these will be revived, as we are constantly becoming more aware of our cultural heritage and our simple past.

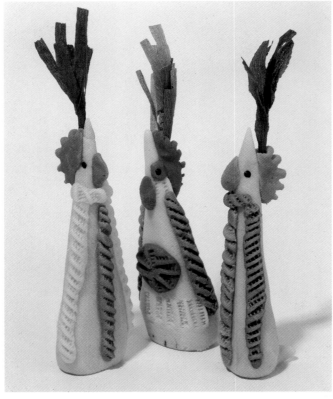

ROOSTERS
3½″ high, Province of Puebla

DOGS
2″ and 4″ long, Province of Puebla

HEN WITH CHICKS
3½" high. Province of Puebla

Many regions or villages in Mexico distinguish themselves through a confectionary style of their own. These animals made from pumpkin seed paste represent the household companions the dead souls take along on their journey to the afterworld. According to Aztec legend, Xoloitzciuntly is the name of the dog who carries these souls across the river and accompanies them on their trip.

ZEBRA AND RAM
6" high. Toluca

A zebra and ram, both made from sugar paste, are among the thousands of sugar animals produced for the festivities of November 1. They are sold at the vast market of alfeñiques in Toluca.

COFFINS AND SKELETONS
3½" long. Puebla

Both the coffins and the skeletons they contain are made of sugar paste and are destined for consumption.

(OPPOSITE) TOY TABLE WITH SKULL
Table: 3" high. Puebla

A miniature wooden table, adorned with real candles and lace, is a replica of the altars prepared in front of the houses in Mexico for the Day of the Dead. The skull, pan de los muertes, and colored fruit are made of sugar.

SUGAR SKULL
4" tall. Puebla

The sugar skull, or calavera, is king of sweets on the Day of the Dead. The majority of skulls are 2 to 3 inches high. They are made of compressed sugar in terra-cotta molds, decorated with royal icing, and carry a paper headband with the name of a beloved person.

BOXES OF HIGASHI CANDY
8 x 8". Kameya Suehiro Shop, Kyoto

THREE TYPES OF SWEETS
Box: 3½ x 9½". Kyoto

A box of higashi candy named Kyo No Yosuga (reminders of Kyoto) takes its inspiration from the changing seasons. Its contents vary according to the time of year it is sold. The fan in the center compartment indicates summertime. The division into the five sections is called "four and a half mats," the mat being a standard measure of Japanese interiors.

An August shopping spree in Kyoto yields an elegant, oblong, wooden box of higashi candy depicting the scenery of that city. The three cinnamon-flavored cookies sprinkled with "medicinal" gold leaf (lower left) were bought as a souvenir near a shrine. The folded packet with tissue wrapper (lower right) is a form of monaka, a bean paste sweet encased in a rice flour wafer.

"GYU HI" BOX WITH THREE FLOWERS
9 x 9". Toraya, Tokyo

A box of fine unpainted wood takes its shape from the traditional stands used for votive offerings. The lotus flower and two chrysanthemums inside are made of a dry type of candy. This expensive item, ordered for funeral and memorial services, is created by the prestigious shop Toraya. The yellow border of the doily and the white string and tassels denote sadness. The same box, when decorated in red and white, contains cranes, turtles, and pine trees (symbols of longevity), and is presented at a wedding or anniversary.

WOODEN CANDY BOX
6½ x 9½", Kyoto

This candy box symbolizes the river and is a delightful example of Japan's love for literal representation. Each row of higashi candy depicts a different stratum of the river's life. From the bottom up are whirlpools, crabs, fish, waves, houseboats, pinecones, bundles of bamboo, plum blossoms, chrysanthemums, and mountains. Sprinkled over the surface are pine needles, maple leaves, fringed blossoms, and a butterfly.

PEONY
6″ diameter. Toraya, Tokyo

One of Japan's most famous flowers is the peony. This life-size specimen is entirely made of sugar paste with the exception of the wire stems which are covered in plastic. It displays the seemingly boundless virtuosity of Japanese confectioners.

MONAKA SWEETS
2½" diameter. Toraya, Tokyo

One of Japan's favorite sweets is monaka, for which white or whole azuki bean jam is sandwiched between rice wafers and then pressed into shapes such as these cherry or plum blossoms. This particular
monaka is named miyo no haru, which means "spring which forever reigns."

(OPPOSITE) CARDBOARD BOX OF CANDY
8½ x 6". Kyoto

This checkered cardboard box bought in the Kyoto market contains various higashi and jelly-type candies in the shape of fruits and flowers. Though less expensive than the sophisticated wooden boxes, this
object is imbued with the same love for symbols and detail as the gifts bought in venerable old stores.

PACKAGED SWEETS OF INTERNATIONAL ORIGIN
Sardine can: 3³/₄ x 4³/₄"

In today's world of sweets, packaging has to a large extent replaced carefully handmade objects. Today, attractive boxes, paper stickers, and colorful foils are mass produced, but they still keep alive symbolic images of hearts and fishes. Old-fashioned labels and typography have joined the ranks of meaningful images, conveying a message of enduring quality.

Selected Bibliography

American Heritage Cookbook and History of American Eating and Drinking. New York, 1964.

Barthes, Roland. *Mythologies.* Paris: Editions du Seuil, 1957.

Baxa, Jacob, and Guntwin Bruhns. *Zucker im Leben der Völker.* Berlin: Verlag Dr. Albert Bartens, 1967.

Brillat-Savarin, Jean-Anthélme. *Physiologie du goût.* Belley, Librairie Gustave Adam, 1948.

Charsley, Simon R. *Wedding Cakes and Cultural History.* London: Rout-ledge, 1992.

Cosman, Madeleine Pelner. *Medieval Holidays and Festivals.* New York: Charles Scribner's Sons, 1981.

Dickson, Paul. *The Great American Ice Cream Book.* New York: Atheneum, 1978.

Evans, Meryle, Sidney M. Mintz, and William Woys Weaver. *Confectioner's Art.* Exh. cat. New York: American Craft Museum, 1988.

Field, Carol. *The Italian Baker.* New York: Harper Collins, 1985.

Friedell, Egon. *Kulturgeschichte der Neuzeit.* Munich: C. H. Beck'sche Verlagsbuchhandlung, 1927, 1931.

Gruber, Carl. *Die Conditorei in Wort und Bild.* Dresden: R. Th. Hauser, 1896.

Hartley, Dorothy. *Food in England.* London: Macdonald & Co. Publishers Ltd., 1954.

Heckmann, A. *Grosses Konditoreibuch.* Nordhausen: Heinrich Killinger Verlagsgesellschaft M.B.H., c. 1910.

Hines, Mary Ann, Gordon Marshall, and William Woys Weaver. *The Larder Invaded.* Exh. cat. Philadelphia: The Library Company of Philadelphia, 1987.

Hübscher, Angelika. *Geniesse mit Casanova.* Zurich: Werner Classen Verlag, 1964.

Huxley, Anthony. *Green Inheritance.* London: Gaia Books Ltd., 1984.

Kaiser, Dolf. *Fast ein Volk von Zuckerbäckern.* Zurich: Verlag Neue Zürcher Zeitung, 1985.

Kaltenbach, Marianne. *Ächti Schwizer Chuchi.* Bern: Hallwag A. G., 1983.

Kunstgeschichte des Backwerks. Oldenburg: Herausgegeben von Hans Jürgen Hansen, Gerhard Stalling Verlag, 1968.

Leitich, Anna Tizia. *Wiener Zuckerbäcker.* Vienna: Amalthea Verlag, 1980.

Marshall, A. B. *The Book of Ices.* Introduced by Barbara Ketchum Wheaton. New York: The Metropolitan Museum of Art, 1976.

McGee, Harold. *On Food and Cooking.* New York: Collier Books, 1984.

Mintz, Sidney W. *Sweetness and Power.* New York: Penguin Books, 1987.

Morton, Monica and Frederic. *Chocolate: An Illustrated History.* New York: Crown Publishers, 1986.

Origo, Iris. *The Merchant of Prato.* London: Jonathan Cape, 1957.

Quayle, Eric. *Old Cook Books.* New York: Dutton, 1978.

Revel, Jean-François. *Culture and Cuisine.* New York: Doubleday, 1982.

Root, Waverly. *Food.* New York: Simon & Schuster, 1980.

———, and Richard de Rochemont. *Eating in America.* New York: The Ecco Press, 1981.

Sheraton, Mimi. *Visions of Sugarplums.* New York: Harper & Row, 1968.

Stallings, W. S., Jr. "Ice Cream and Water Ices in 17th and 18th Century England." *Petit Propos Culinaires* 3 Supplement (London: July 1985).

Stellingwerf. *The Gingerbread Book.* London: Charles Letts & Co. Ltd., 1991.

Sucre d'Art. Exh. cat. Paris: Musée des Arts Decoratifs, 1978.

Tannahill, Reay. *Food in History.* New York: Stein & Day, 1973.

Traité de Patisserie, Confiserie d'apres la Methode Professionelle. Chalon-sur-Saône: Felix Prost, 1947.

Weaver, William Woys. *America Eats: Forms of American Folk Art.* New York: Harper & Row, 1989.

Weiner, Piroska. *Geschnitzte Lebkuchenformen in Ungarn.* Budapest: Corvina Verlag, 1964.

Wheaton, Barbara Ketchum. *Savoring the Past.* Philadelphia: The University of Pennsylvania Press, 1983.

Acknowledgments

Above all I would like to thank Paul Gottlieb for his positive response when I showed him the first confectionary pictures more than a decade ago and for publishing them now that the project has grown to the size of this book. At Harry N. Abrams, Inc., I am equally indebted to my editor, Ruth Peltason, for her enthusiasm and steady support, and for wrestling with my prose; and to Dana Sloan for her sensitive and elegant design.

Many thanks to Nancy Harmon Jenkins for her list of people to talk to and books to read. I also much appreciated the generous advice and helpful suggestions given to me by Mimi Sheraton, Meryle Evans, William Woys Weaver, and by Nach Waxman, from Kitchen, Arts and Letters bookstore. Further heartfelt thanks go to Carol Professional Color Lab in New York for years of fine work and excellent service.

And last but not least I would like to express my gratitude to my friends who kept me supplied with sweets and enthusiasm all along or who helped in other constructive ways: Evelyn Hofer, Aline Aluja, Jose Ramon Aluja, Midori Nishizawa, Elizabeth Novick, Lana Ping Jokel, Inigo della Huerta, Ursula Schinz, Jimmy Rubin, Jackie Moncada, Gordon Foster, Kasmin, Jean-Pierre Blancpain, Hedwig Zellweger, Lisette Bruderer, Noa Zanolli Davenport, Rene Burgauer, Christian Kurz, Thomas Dubs, Vroni Fierz, Tessa Traeger, Patrick Kinmonth, Bridget De Socio, Mark Lyon, and Renate Legewie. Their participation has made this book a sheer pleasure to work on.

Marina Schinz
New York, 1994

EDITOR: Ruth A. Peltason
DESIGNER: Dana Sloan

Library of Congress Cataloging-in-Publication Data
Schinz, Marina.
The book of sweets / Marina Schinz.
p.   cm.
ISBN 0–8109–3131–1
1. Desserts.   I. Title
TX773.S332   1994
641.8′6—dc20   94–1545